I0142199

Relax: It's Just SAT Writing

A Comprehensive Study Guide to Mastering the Writing Portions of the SAT

Daniel Sullivan

Lexington Park, Maryland

Copyright © 2013 Daniel Sullivan

All rights reserved.

ISBN 978-0-578-12213-7

First Edition, 2013

Document Layout: Mark Jude Sullivan
Editorial Support: Laura Friel

SAT is a registered trademark of the College Board,
which neither sponsors nor endorses this product.

DEDICATION

Sister Saint Dorothy, OSF

CONTENTS

ACKNOWLEDGMENTS

I want to thank all my former students at St. Mary's Ryken High School in Leonardtown, Maryland, for helping me grow as a teacher. I would also like to thank my current students Reema Patel, Sohum Shah, Aman Kankaria, and Rohan Kankaria whose dedication and industry motivate me to do my best. Photographs of these students from Great Mills High School in Great Mills, Maryland, appear throughout the book.

I would also like to express my appreciation to Laura Friel for her editorial assistance and to Minah Kim, Max Choi, Karlo Santos, and Ashley Mae Mangalindan-Santos whose photographs also appear in *Relax: It's Just SAT Writing*.

Finally, Mark Jude Sullivan deserves a special thanks for the book's layout. The conversion of the author's manuscript to a camera-ready copy was onerous and time-consuming. His work made my work easy on the eye and easier to understand.

"Good writers have good sentences in their ears."[1]

---

[1] Adapted from the statement, "have good sentences in your ears," by Jane Kenyon, quoted by Samuel Cohen, editor, *50 Essays: A Portable Anthology.*

AUTHOR'S NOTE

Welcome! Getting ready for the SAT can be stressful, but working carefully through *Relax: It's Just SAT Writing*—its short title is *Relax I*—will relieve some of that stress and help you do your best on the SAT's writing sections.[1]

Doing well on the exam's writing sections is a very specific goal. In a year or two, the SAT will be a thing of the past, and your attention will be on much bigger issues in college. Still, mastering the elements of style and grammar that I'll go over with you in this book will serve you well not only in your final years of high school but also in college and beyond. If you apply to your own writing what we cover during our work together, you'll become a more careful writer and a better editor of your own work. More immediately, your mastery of the points of grammar and style that we'll cover in *Relax I* will increase your SAT score.

Those are not just idle claims. I believe in this book. It's the result of what I've learned from hundreds of hours of tutoring high school students as they prepare for the SAT as well as thousands of hours of teaching high school and college English courses.

That may sound like boasting, and you probably find braggarts to be "royal pains," just as I do. I mention my experience only to assure you that I've worked with high school students for a number of years and that I've seen what works and what doesn't. I ask only that you give *Relax I* an honest chance. If you do, I think you'll be pleased with the results.

You've probably noticed that in this introduction I've used contractions, for example, "I've," "you've," and "you're" in place of their formal counterparts. I've also used colloquial expressions

---

[1] *Relax: It's Just SAT Writing* is the first of three planned SAT study guides: the second will cover math, and the third will prepare you for the SAT's critical reading sections.

and informal diction.[1] You wouldn't use contractions or informal diction in an assignment for your English class, so why do I use them here?

I want the tone of this book to be more conversational than academic. You already have enough textbooks. My approach doesn't mean that I'm "dumbing anything down" for you. This approach simply reflects the way I speak when I tutor students for the SAT. It's simply the way we talk—even about serious topics.

In *Relax I*, I've tried to strike a balance between being serious about important subject matter, such as the SAT, and approaching the material in a relaxed way. As an American high school student, you're already under enough pressure. You're probably hearing or saying to yourself, far too often, "You've got to do well on the SAT!" "Get a move on, will you? Those college applications aren't going to mail themselves." "You've got to take more AP courses if you expect to get into Georgetown University." "From the way she's been acting, I think Emma Woodhouse is going to dump me."

I've said enough. Take a deep breath. Let's begin.

---

[1] You'll also notice that I split infinitives and end clauses with prepositions in *Relax I*. I'll go over the justification in the appendix on style.

PART I: THE SAT'S MULTIPLE-CHOICE WRITING SECTION

Some of you may have already taken the SAT or completed SAT practice tests. Still, let's review how the test is put together for those who are new to SAT preparation.

The exam begins with an essay assignment, which counts for about thirty percent of your total writing score. The essay is followed by math problems and then the first of several reading comprehension sections. There will be more math problems, and then you face the exam's second writing section that asks you to identify errors in grammar and style and to select the best option for writing a sentence or parts of a student's essay. The exam then presents more math problems, more reading comprehension passages, and, finally, more sentences to be evaluated for proper style and grammar. The second and third writing sections of the exam are in multiple-choice format and are worth about 560 points.

As my students and I have worked through a number of SAT practice tests, I've noticed that the same points of grammar and style keep appearing in the multiple-choice sections. By my count, there are eighteen errors that recur on the SAT practice tests. It's no coincidence that these are the same mistakes that appear most frequently in high school and college writing. Here are the eighteen worst offenders that we'll cover in *Relax I*:

1. Misplaced Modifiers
2. Wordiness
3. Sentence Fragments
4. Comma Splices and Run-On Sentences
5. Errors with Double Negatives
6. The "Between-You-and I" Error
7. Unclear Pronoun References

LESSON 1: MISPLACED MODIFIERS

Modifiers are words or groups of words that give us information about other words in a sentence—the subject, the verb, the object, and so on. Modifiers can come in the form of single words such as adjectives or adverbs. For instance, when I write, "Emma is wearing a <u>black</u> dress," I'm using a modifier—in this case the adjective "black"—to give information about her dress. If I say, "Kaycee walked <u>slowly</u> into the room," I'm using the adverb "slowly," another kind of modifier, to give information about the verb, namely, how she walked into the room. So far, I haven't said anything complicated or earth-shattering about modifiers. Let's move on.

Modifiers also come in the form of phrases or clauses. Look at the following sentences:

> **A.** <u>Unable to complete any of the exercises</u>, Wendel was cut from the team.

> **B.** <u>Hobbled by a sprained ankle</u>, the first-string quarterback on my fantasy team will be inactive for next Sunday's game.

In Sentence A, "unable to complete any of the exercises," is a phrase that modifies "Wendell." It gives us information about one of the main reasons that Wendell didn't make the team. In Sentence B, "hobbled by a sprained ankle," is a phrase that modifies "the first-string quarterback" and gives us information about his status for next Sunday's game.

In some cases, modifiers can modify or give information about other modifiers. For example, the statement, "his smile was <u>barely</u> perceptible," contains two modifiers: 1. "perceptible," an adjective, which tells something about the smile, and 2. "barely," an adverb, which modifies "perceptible," and tells us to what degree his smile was noticeable. Make a mental note that modifiers such as adverbs can modify other modifiers, for instance, adjectives. Improperly modifying an adjective is one of the errors we'll cover in Lesson 11.

There's one more kind of modifier that I'd like to go over with you: the subordinate clause. Consider the following sentence that has two subordinate clauses: "Kevin, my son-in-law, <u>who is the commissioner of our fantasy football league</u>, benched his starting quarterback, <u>who has a sprained ankle</u>." The two subordinate clauses give us information about the nouns they modify. "Who is the commissioner of our fantasy football league," is a modifier that gives us information about Kevin. The clause, "who sprained his ankle," gives us information about Kevin's starting quarterback.

Up to this point, we've reviewed different kinds of modifiers, but what is a "misplaced modifier," which is an error frequently made in writing? The name says it all. It's a modifier that's been placed in the wrong part of a sentence.

Keep in mind that when a writer composes a sentence, he or she has to be careful about where to place modifiers. Proper placement of a modifier conveys meaning; *mis*placing a modifier distorts it. Look at the placement of the modifier "only" in the following sentences. In each case, *where* "only" is placed completely changes the meaning.

I eat **only** eggs for breakfast.

The placement of "only" before "eggs" means that I eat eggs and nothing else for breakfast. I imagine that eating just eggs would get rather boring after a while, but that's what the sentence means.

> **Only** I eat eggs for breakfast.

In this sentence, the placement of "only"—before "I"—means that I'm the only person who eats eggs for breakfast. That's quite a claim, but we know it's not factual, and the inaccuracy is simply the result of the sloppy placement of the word, "only."

> I eat eggs **only** for breakfast.

In this sentence, the placement of "only" before the phrase "for breakfast" means that I will eat eggs for breakfast but at no other time.

> I **only** eat eggs for breakfast.

In this sentence, the placement of "only" before the verb "eat" is ambiguous. It can mean that I do one thing and only one thing: eat eggs. I do nothing else but eat eggs. I don't study, I don't text my best friend, I don't go to school, I don't check Facebook. The only thing I ever do is to eat eggs. What a life!

Someone will no doubt think, "Give me a break! I know what the writer means. You're being picky, just like all English teachers."

All right, let's look at the following example to demonstrate that where we place a modifier in a sentence is important, and a modifier's location means something very specific. Some of the funniest sentences in English occur when a writer, unintentionally, places a modifier in the wrong place. Look at this sentence:

> **Able to consume an entire colony of insects at one meal**, **Ms. Shandy**, our biology teacher, showed us slides of an African anteater.

Wow! By placing the modifier (in this case a phrase) "able to consume an entire colony of insects at one meal" next to "Ms. Shandy, our biology teacher," the writer is actually saying that Ms. Shandy eats lots of insects at one sitting and not necessarily the strange-looking animal from Africa. If that's the case, then Ms. Shandy deserves special recognition, but what the writer meant to do, no doubt, is to place the modifier next to the thing it describes — the African anteater. Here's the correction in which the modifier is put in its proper place in the sentence:

> Ms. Shandy, our biology teacher, showed us slides of an *African anteater*, [which is] *able to consume an entire colony of insects at one meal.*

The point of all this is that writers have to be careful about **where** to place individual parts of their sentences. Carelessly placing modifiers in sentences can result in some unintentionally ludicrous[1] expressions.

Dangling[2] or Misplaced Participles

Before we move on to the next lesson, "Wordiness," we need to examine a specialized kind of misplaced modifier—the dangling participle. A "participle" is a form of the verb that acts like an adjective. Most often, a participle describes **an action and can take an object.** (A bit later in this lesson, we'll look at participles formed from linking verbs. Obviously, linking verbs don't take objects, but they do have complements—adjectives or nouns that give information about the subject of the sentence or clause—but more about that later.)

---

[1] "Ludicrous" is a great SAT word. Look it up and make a file card for the word noting its part of speech and its definition.

[2] Students have been making sport of the term "dangling participle" for generations. A dangling participle is simply one special type of a misplaced modifier.

Consider this sentence:

> "**Seeing** the Grand Canyon for the first time, **I** was speechless."

In this example, "Seeing" is a participle, it's a form of the verb "to see," it involves an action, and it modifies the pronoun "I." Besides all that, the participle "seeing" also takes an object—"the Grand Canyon." When a participle is carelessly placed in a sentence, we encounter a common but **egregious**[1] grammatical mistake. There's one more point to remember about participles— and this one is probably the most important. Since many participles are taken from action verbs AND since a participle acts like an adjective, the participle can modify only a noun or pronoun referring to someone or something that can actually perform the action.

Consider the following example:

> **Driving** through Yosemite National Park, **it** was clear to us that many campsites had been littered with garbage, which would surely attract brown bears, coyotes, and rodents.

"Driving" in this sentence is a participle and part of the phrase that the writer has placed next to the word "it." But who did the driving? "We" or "it"? *We* did of course, so the modifier, the participle, is misplaced, and the sentence has to be rearranged, that is, the participle has to be put as closely as possible to "we," who can actually do the driving.

---

[1] "Egregious" is another great SAT word. I will shade other words that you'd do well to make note cards for and record their definitions. Whatever you do, please do NOT be the person who calls out to a college roommate, "hey, what does 'jejune' mean?" Get into the habit of using a dictionary. You certainly don't want to sound like a slacker by asking someone, "hey, how do you spell 'abscond'?"

Driving through Yosemite National Park, *we noticed that* many campsites had been littered with garbage, which would surely attract brown bears, coyotes, and rodents.

Let's look at another example of a misplaced (its legal name is "dangling") participle:

Driving through Yosemite National Park, **many littered campsites**, we felt, would attract brown bears, coyotes, and rodents.

It's fairly clear how badly this sentence is put together. The position of the participial phrase, "driving through Yosemite National Park," namely, close to "campsites," makes it sound as if the campsites were doing the driving.

We have to keep in mind that participles involve action, yet they act like adjectives, we have to look at the noun or pronoun that the participle modifies. Does the noun or pronoun refer to someone or something that can actually perform the action? If it doesn't, then you have a dangling participle, the sentence is unacceptable, and the sentence must be rewritten.

Look at the following dangling or misplaced participle:

Looking through our new telescope, **the stars** resembled small diamonds.

In this sentence, "looking" is a participle, and it modifies "the stars." From the way the sentence is put together, "the stars" were the ones using the telescope. To correct the error, we need to reword the sentence in this way:

Looking through our new telescope, *we* thought that the stars resembled small diamonds.

Finally, I mentioned that I would have something to say about the participles of linking verbs such as those that don't involve action.

(The most common linking verbs are: "be," "become," "look," "appear," "sound," "taste," "smell," and "feel.") While the participles of these verbs don't involve action or take direct objects, they still tell us something about the nouns they modify. The participles of linking verbs can also be badly misplaced in a sentence. Consider the following sentence:

Smelling bad, **we** refused to eat the oysters.

We don't really need to analyze that sentence, do we?

So don't misplace your modifiers or dangle your participles in your own writing, and be able to identify misplaced modifiers, as you move through the SAT's multiple-choice grammar and style sections. If you're ever in doubt, think of our dedicated biology teacher, Ms. Shandy, and the African anteater. Let's move on to "wordiness," a frequent problem in writing.

STUDY AID

Make NOTE CARDS of unfamiliar vocabulary words.
Include the word, its part of speech, and meaning.

Side One:

JEJUNE

adj.

Side Two:

---

1. naive, simplistic, and superficial: "their entirely predictable and usually jejune opinions."

2. (of ideas or writings) dry and uninteresting: "the poem seems to me rather jejune."

[NOTE: All definitions cited in *Relax I*, unless otherwise noted, are taken from the *New Oxford American Dictionary*.]

LESSON 2: WORDINESS

My office is a mess. Everywhere you look there are notes and papers that I don't need any more. Many of the things that I do need I can't find because they're misplaced or buried beneath the clutter. My messy office is a lot like a piece of writing that's been hastily or carelessly written: there's lots of clutter—unnecessary words, needless repetitions, and useless expressions all of which can hide the actual meaning. In contrast, straightening up my office is like careful editing and re-writing: I get rid of the things that I don't need and put the things that I intend to keep in their proper places. You won't be expected to rewrite[1] poorly written passages on the SAT. But in several of the writing sections, you will be presented with variations of a sentence and asked to choose the most effective version, one that is clear, concise and error-free. Often, the options contain wordy expressions, so you'll need to be alert to spot and eliminate them from consideration.

Let's look at some examples of wordy expressions.

If I were to write, "Mr. Olon is the one assigned by the principal to teach the American Literature course at our high school," you would obviously know what I meant, but the writing is wordy. Out of the sentence's nineteen words, a number of them are unnecessary. In other words, the sentence has too much clutter.

_____

[1] Yes, I just split an infinitive. In the "Appendix on Style," I'll present a case for splitting infinitives and ending clauses with prepositions. (I can already hear the murmurings of some of the "grammar prudes" who are just itching for a debate on those two subjects. Be patient. We'll answer those objections soon enough.)

Here's a revision of that sentence without the original version's unnecessary words:

> Mr. Olon teaches American Literature at our high school.

The revision says the same thing as does the wordy original, but the revision is more direct and contains ten fewer words. Here's a rule of thumb when comparing two versions of a piece of writing: if you can write a sentence in fewer words, without changing the meaning, or introducing any grammatical errors, then prefer the shorter version. If one were to object to my revision of the original and claim that being assigned to teach American Literature by the principal is an important part of the intended meaning, the sentence can still be cleaned up and improved:

> The principal assigned Mr. Olon to teach American Literature at our high school.

The revision removes clutter and saves six words.

Here's an example of a wordy paragraph:

> The U.S. Constitution sets up the authority for the three branches of the U.S. government, which are the executive, the legislative, and the judicial branches of our national government. Where that authority is found for these three branches of the national government is in the first three Articles of the Constitution. The first three Articles list the powers of the officials in each branch and what qualifies them for the jobs as well as what exactly their duties are. (79 words)

Wow! The following revision removes the original's needless words and redundancies and corrects its illogic:

> The first three Articles of the U.S. Constitution authorize, respectively, the executive, legislative, and judicial branches of our national government. Each of these

Articles lists the powers, qualifications, and duties of the officials who serve in that branch. (38 words)

Let's look at another example of wordiness:

In view of the fact that home buying is one of the most important economic decisions you will ever make in your lifetime, one thing to ask your mortgage banker that should be asked before any other question is what is the mortgage's interest rate and whether or not the rate is fixed or variable. (55 words)

Why would anyone waste so many words to introduce simple questions for potential homebuyers to ask a mortgage banker? First, "in view of the fact that" is a long-winded way of saying, "because." Is the phrase "in his or her lifetime" necessary? At what other time would one buy a home, if not during one's lifetime? Look at the next part of the sentence:

...one thing to ask your mortgage banker that should be asked before any other question...

"One thing to ask" is a question, and if the question is to be asked "before any other question," what is it other than the "first" question? I would make one final adjustment. Since there are actually two questions that the writer mentions—what is the interest rate and what kind of rate applies—fixed or variable— then the sentence should read "questions." Without the clutter of the original sentence, an acceptable revision looks like this:

Because home buying is one of the most important economic decisions that you will ever make, the first questions you should ask your mortgage banker are what is the interest rate and whether the rate is fixed or variable. (39 words)

The sum of our discussion on wordiness is that if you can communicate your ideas clearly, concisely, logically, and correctly, you will be on your way to being an accomplished writer. Of course, it wouldn't hurt if your sentences occasionally express your ideas with eloquence or wit, but your primary goal in expository writing is to be clear, concise, and correct.

What Being Concise Does NOT Mean

During the Clinton Administration, I did some writing for the government, and, at the time, there was a laudable effort to make government writing clear to the average person. For years, most people had a hard time understanding government writing because it was so wordy and filled with jargon, so the effort to make government writing clearer was a welcome one. The thought behind this "plain-language" effort was that since the work of government is to serve the public, then the public should be able to understand what the government has to say; otherwise, the writing is useless. I was delighted with this approach. I recall one unknown government writer—most government writers are anonymous since they are ghostwriters for higher-ranking officials—cautioned us that this plain-writing initiative did not mean that we were to reduce our writing to grunts or to "Me-Tarzan, You-Jane" statements. That's not the kind of brevity we sought back then, nor is it the kind of conciseness we're after now.

LESSON 3: SENTENCE FRAGMENTS

Here are two definitions that the *New Oxford American Dictionary* gives for a fragment: "a small part broken or separated off something..." and "an isolated or incomplete part of something." The name of this kind of grammatical error describes clearly what's at stake: a sentence fragment is a word or a group of words that is only an incomplete part of a sentence. When we read a sentence fragment, it's obvious that something is missing, that what we have in front of us has been separated from something larger, and the smaller piece doesn't make complete sense.

There are two things to keep in mind about sentence fragments. First, a sentence fragment looks like a sentence; it is punctuated as if it were a sentence. The first word in a sentence fragment is capitalized, and a period follows the last word. Second, a sentence fragment puzzles us as readers and leaves us wanting and needing more information to make any sense out of what we just read. In other words, a sentence fragment is trying to pass itself off as if it were a sentence, but it's only a part or a fragment of something larger, and it's obvious that something's missing.

Here are several examples of sentence fragments:

In the beginning.

Although *Tom Jones* isn't on our reading list.

Because Shakespeare's family had financial difficulties.

We obviously need more information to make any sense out of these sentence fragments. In the first example, "In the beginning," we ask ourselves a number of questions: what about the beginning? who's involved? what happened? what's going to happen? You get the idea. There are just too many details left out, yet the phrase is punctuated as if it were a sentence. The fragment has to be corrected in order that we may have a complete sentence. In the second example, "Although *Tom Jones* isn't on our reading list," we're expecting a contrast of some sort, but we're left hanging and don't get the information to help us make sense out of what we just read. This group of words creates what I call the "huh?" factor. After reading it, a sensible response would probably be, "huh?" The same thing goes for the last example. We have a cause, "Because Shakespeare's family had financial difficulties," but we don't have an effect or a result, namely, what happened to Shakespeare or his family. Again, we're left puzzled and asking ourselves, "huh?" or "what about the family's financial difficulties?"

The "huh?" factor has its limitations. It can be useful for detecting sentence fragments. But the "huh?" factor is misused if we dismiss a passage simply because we're puzzled when we first read it. Sometimes, even the best writing stymies us, and I mean *all* of us, including English teachers. If we respond with "huh?" to a piece of writing, we need to decide whether the expression is difficult or incomplete. If the expression is difficult to understand, then we owe it to ourselves to read the passage again so that we can understand and own it. If the expression reflects a fragmented thought, then we've uncovered a sentence "fraud," something we'll need to spot on the SAT and something we'll need to avoid in our own writing. Practically speaking, complex-but-complete sentences will not appear on the multiple-choice parts of the SAT's writing assessment.

As a self-check to decide whether what appears to be a sentence really is one, and not a fragment, **first**, locate the subject in the

main clause. (Any group of words that begins with a subordinating conjunction, namely, "although," "because," "when," "since," etc., is not a main clause. It is a subordinate or dependent clause, one that can't stand on its own and, by itself, doesn't express a complete thought.) **Second**, identify the main verb. If you have both a subject and a main verb in an independent clause—one that can stand on its own, one that makes complete sense—then you have a sentence.

Remember that if an incomplete form of the verb is used instead of a "main verb," it's still a fragment. Here's another example:

John **auditioning** for the role of Falstaff.

That's clearly not a sentence, but rather a sentence fragment because there's no main verb. To correct the fragment, we would need a complete verb form, such as in the following sentences:

John *is auditioning* for the role of Falstaff.

John *auditioned* for the role of Falstaff.

John *will be auditioning* for the role of Falstaff.

To review, let's look one last time at some examples of sentence fragments, and how we can correct them to express complete thoughts:

We **registering** for Dr. Wagner's British Novel course. [Fragment—there's no correct main verb form.]

We *will be registering* for Dr. Wagner's British Novel course. [Correction—the verb is now complete.]

Although Harry has registered for Dr. Jack Wagner's Shakespeare course. [Huh?]

In the last example, there's no clause that can stand on its own, and we can't make any sense out of what is punctuated as a sentence. We don't know what the outcome of Harry's registration for the course will be. Here's a correction of the last fragment:

> Although Harry has registered for Dr. Jack Wagner's Shakespeare course, *he will still have to take two more three-credit courses this semester*. [Correction—the independent clause, "he will still have to take two more three-credit courses this semester," completes the thought.]

Pace yourself.
Carefully complete just one of Relax I's *lessons each day, and, in less than three weeks, you will have completed your preparation for the grammar and style points tested on the SAT.*

LESSON 4: COMMA SPLICES AND RUN-ON SENTENCES

Comma splices and run-on sentences are "repeat offenders" in academic and professional writing, so there's a good chance that you'll encounter them on the SAT. In two sections of the exam, you'll be shown five versions of a sentence, and you'll have to choose the best version. Let's review comma splices and run-on sentences to increase your chances of spotting them on the test and to avoid them in your own writing.

What exactly are comma splices and run-on sentences?

Comma splices and run-on sentences are so much alike that, in my tutoring, I mention them in virtually the same breath. There are a number of similarities between them so such an approach makes sense.

A comma splice is a punctuation error in which two independent clauses are joined by a comma. (An independent clause, as we mentioned earlier, is one that makes complete sense, can "stand on its own two feet," and doesn't need anything else to complete the thought.)

Here's an example of a comma splice:

> Dr. Wagner's British Novel course was enjoyable, I've registered for his Elizabethan Drama course.

In this example, two independent clauses that are completely understandable by themselves—"Dr. Wagner's British Novel course was enjoyable," and "I've registered for his Elizabethan Drama course"—are joined by a comma.

The **first** way to correct this punctuation error is to separate the two independent clauses with a **semicolon (;)**. Here's the correction:

> Dr. Wagner's British Novel course was *enjoyable; I've* registered for his Elizabethan Drama course.

The **second** way to correct a comma splice is to end the sentence after the first independent clause with a **period** and start a new sentence, for example:

> Dr. Wagner's British Novel course was *enjoyable.* *I've* registered for his Elizabethan Drama course.

The **third** way to correct a comma splice is to join the two independent clauses with a **conjunction**,[1] for instance:

> Dr. Wagner's British Novel course was *enjoyable, so I've* registered for his Elizabethan Drama course.

The **fourth** way is to show the relationship between the two thoughts—in this case, **a cause-effect connection**:

> *Because* Dr. Wagner's British Novel course was *enjoyable,* *I've* registered for his Elizabethan Drama course.

---

[1] When joining two independent clauses with these conjunctions: *for, and, nor, but, or, yet, so,* put **a comma** before the conjunction. As a memory aid, think of these conjunctions as the FANBOYS. When joining two independent clauses with these conjunctions: *however, nevertheless, therefore, otherwise, consequently, moreover,* put **a semicolon before** the conjunction and **a comma after** it.

The comma splice's fraternal twin is the run-on sentence. It's also a punctuation error in which two independent clauses are "run together" or fused into one sentence without any punctuation at all. Look at the following example:

> Dr. Wagner's British Novel course was enjoyable I am looking forward to his Elizabethan Drama course.

To correct a run-on or fused sentence, we make the same changes in punctuation that we did for comma splices, for example:

> Dr. Wagner's British Novel course was *enjoyable; I've* registered for his Elizabethan Drama course.

> Dr. Wagner's British Novel course was *enjoyable. I've* registered for his Elizabethan Drama course.

> Dr. Wagner's British Novel course was *enjoyable, so I've* registered for his Elizabethan Drama course.

> *Because* Dr. Wagner's British Novel course was *enjoyable, I've* registered for his Elizabethan Drama course.

STUDY AID

- Document your reading.

- Record what you read on note cards.

- Include a summary, the theme, a quotation from the reading, and your own personal observation about the material.

It'll help you prepare for writing the SAT Essay. I'll say more about that later.

"Shooting an Elephant" (an essay), George Orwell

SUMMARY: The narrator was a colonial police officer in Burma. He killed an elephant, not because the animal was dangerous, but because the Burmese wanted and expected him to kill it.

THEME: Under pressure from others, people can do disturbing things that are against their beliefs.

QUOTATION: "And suddenly I realized that I should have to shoot the elephant after all. The people expected it of me and I had got to do it; I could feel their two thousand wills pressing me forward, irresistibly."

PERSONAL OBSERVATION: What's disturbing about the narrator's lack of courage is that he killed the elephant because people expected it AND because he didn't want to look like a fool. WOW! That's chilling.

LESSON 5: ERRORS WITH DOUBLE NEGATIVES

In the sentence, "it is not uncommon for high school students to apply to at least two colleges," there are two negatives: "not" and "uncommon." We know that two negatives make a positive, and the meaning of this sentence—"it is not uncommon for high school students to apply to at least two colleges"—is clear: it's fairly typical for high school students to apply to more than one college. In other words, that's what many high school seniors do. In this sentence, I don't use statistics to back up my claim but rely on common knowledge: we know from our experience that a high school senior often applies to at least two colleges or universities, namely, the student's "first-choice" school—the school he or she "really" wants to go to—and also the so-called "safe school," the one that the student believes will be a cinch to get into. If anyone bristles at the previous sentence because I just ended the relative clause with a preposition "to" and the sentence itself with the preposition "into," look at the alternative: "**…'safe school' is the one into which the student believes will be a cinch to get.**" Does anyone with an ounce of common sense really want me to follow the "rule" and write the preceding monstrosity? I rest my case.

I might also say or write, "it's not unreasonable for you to think that way." My use of the double negative—"not" and "unreasonable"—expresses the idea that it's actually reasonable for you to think in a certain way. But why on earth would I use this double negative deliberately? One reason is to offer a concession to someone, that is, to throw someone a bone in a debate or a discussion when we don't agree on a point. My sentence says in effect, "you've got a good point. It's reasonable for you to think that way, but I'm going to give you evidence and reasons that show you why my position is better." These two examples are deliberate double negatives that are perfectly acceptable. There are, however, **faulty double negatives** that are likely candidates to appear on the SAT. Know them because you may have to identify them on the exam and, in some cases, choose corrections for them. Consider these sentences:

A. The students **couldn't scarcely** contain their enthusiasm.
B. She **doesn't hardly** study for exams.
C. They **rarely never** clean up their front yard.
D. There's **hardly no** snow on the ground.
E. They couldn't go anywhere **without no** car.

"Hardly," "rarely," "scarcely," and "barely," are already negatives; "couldn't," "no," "without," and "never" are too, so we don't need a second negative to communicate a negative meaning. Here then are the correct versions of the preceding faulty sentences:

A. The students *could scarcely* contain their enthusiasm.
B. She *hardly ever* goes to the school's football games.
C. They *rarely ever* clean up their front yard.
D. There's *hardly any* snow on the ground.
E. They couldn't go anywhere *without a* car.

LESSON 6: THE BETWEEN-YOU-AND-I ERROR

As we're growing up and learning English (as well as for those whose first language is not English but who have gained mastery of the language), we can sense when something is strange, out of place, or expressed incorrectly in our language. Linguists call this capability "competence grammar." We know that a sentence like, "James saw she at the poetry reading" is wrong. Likewise, when we hear, "Him saw her at the bookstore," we know that that's simply not acceptable, basic English. No English teacher has to point that out to us. We simply know that the pronoun "him" is incorrect. There are other situations in which grammatical errors are not as clear, especially when people who should know better make the mistake.

There are far too many people (celebrities, talk-show hosts, news anchors on television, and others who should know better) who misuse the first person pronoun "I" in the following ways:

> My fans' support of **my family and I** after the L.A.P.D.'s phony shoplifting charge has touched me deeply.

> The Chairman of the English Department invited **my wife and I** to her dinner party.

> The President of our company spoke with **my supervisor and I** about the decrease in sales.

> The difference between **Tom and I** is that Tom has already

satisfied all of his course requirements for graduation.

In each of these examples, the pronoun "I" is misused.

Undoubtedly, people mistakenly think that "I" sounds more refined and more polite than plain, old "me." In the back of many people's minds, "I" belongs at a dinner party with the Chairman of the English Department and listening to classical music—while "me" belongs under the chassis of a car doing work on the exhaust system. "Me," however, is a perfectly fine word when it's used correctly, but the way people misuse these pronouns, you'd think that "I" has made it in the world while "me" does all the dirty work and is a second-class citizen. In each of the cases above, however, the writer or the speaker is being overly—and incorrectly— proper or refined. Theodore M. Bernstein, author of *The Careful Writer: A Modern Guide to English Usage*, coins the word "overrefinement" to describe the "between-you-and-I" error. The authors of the previous examples are trying far too hard to sound proper. They're putting on airs and trying to convince their readers or listeners that they're elegant—efforts that are completely unnecessary and actually incorrect. I like to think of the "between-you-and-I" error as a young man who wears a suit to a beach party, or a woman who wears an evening gown to the library: neither the suit nor the evening gown is appropriate for the occasion. The suit may look great, the evening gown may be stunning, but they're out of place at the beach or the library, and when you think about it, they would look a little ridiculous in those circumstances. Yes, they're cheesy analogies, but if they help you avoid the error that our celebrities, our politicians, and news professionals continue to make, then these silly analogies have done their job.

Here are corrections of the previous examples:

> My fans' support of *my family and me* after the L.A.P.D.'s phony shoplifting charge has been touching.

The Chairman of the English Department invited *my wife and me* to her dinner party.

The President of our company spoke with *my supervisor and me* about the decrease in sales.

The difference between *Tom and me* is that Tom has actually satisfied all of his course requirements for graduation.

If you're ever uncertain whether something like, "toward my family and I" is an error or not, just remove the first part of the phrase—in this case "my family." Now read the sentence, "My fans' support toward I after the L.A.P.D.'s phony shoplifting charge has been touching." You obviously have your answer. "Toward I" sounds ridiculous, so change "I" to "me" and put "my family" back into the picture. Now the sentence is correct:

My fans' support of my family and *me* after the L.A.P.D.'s phony shoplifting charge has been touching.

Let me offer one final thought about the "between-you-and-I" error. As you are working your way through the SAT, red flags should start waving when you see a personal pronoun underlined in one of the test's multiple-choice writing sections. Take a careful look at any underlined phrase that contains some form of the **personal pronouns**—*I, you, he, she, it, we, you,* or *they*. Does the pronoun follow[1] a verb or a preposition, especially "between"? If so, then the pronoun must be in this form—*me, her, him, us,* or *them*—which we call the "objective case."

In summary, when dealing with personal pronouns on the SAT, remember to be on the lookout an "I" that should be a "me."

---

[1] To simplify matters, I use the terms *follow* rather than the "object of a verb or preposition" and *in this form* instead of "objective case."

STUDY AID

ARMED and DANGEROUS:
ENGLISH GRAMMAR'S WORST OFFENDERS

1. Misplaced Modifiers
2. Wordiness
3. Sentence Fragments
4. Comma Splices and Run-On Sentences
5. Errors with Double Negatives
6. The "Between-You-and I" Error
7. Unclear Pronoun References
8. Inconsistent Pronoun References
9. Faulty Comparisons
10. The "2-is-not-1" Error
11. Mistakes with Adverbs and Adjectives
12. "Who" vs. "Whom"
13. Errors with Verb Tenses
14. Lack of Agreement of a Verb with its Subject
15. Lack of Agreement of a Pronoun with its Antecedent
16. Lack of Parallelism
17. Mistakes with Idioms and Diction
18. Relatives...Which...That...Who

LESSON 7: UNCLEAR PRONOUN REFERENCES

Consider this sentence:

> Jim never studied. He broke every one of the rules in his
> dormitory, and he harassed other students. **It** was clearly
> the reason the university expelled him after only one
> semester.

The writer of that short passage may know what "it" refers to in
the second sentence, but "it" isn't clear at all. What was the reason
that Jim was expelled? There are four candidates—failing to study,
breaking rules, harassing others, or all three of these problems
in combination—that caused his expulsion. The reason is probably
a combination of all three asinine behaviors, but to clear up the
uncertainty, the precise writer has to be specific. Here is a
correction of the unclear pronoun reference "it":

> Jim never studied. He broke every one of the rules in his
> dormitory, and he harassed other students. *His immaturity*
> was clearly the reason the university expelled him after
> only one semester.

"His immaturity" is a good summary of all three behaviors and
therefore a clear replacement for the unclear "it."

Here's another example of an unclear personal pronoun.
Remember that pronouns take the place of nouns, and sometimes

other pronouns, so when we compose sentences there can't be any doubt about what we're referring to; otherwise, there's confusion and possible misinterpretation— two enemies of effective communication.

Let's now look at an example of an unclear demonstrative pronoun reference. (Demonstrative pronouns point to things. "*That* is my book, not yours!" "*This* is the best novel I've ever read.") Here are two sentences; the second contains an unclear demonstrative pronoun reference:

> While Jim wasn't looking, someone stole his wallet. **That** caused him untold problems since he was stranded in a strange city without a driver's license, credit cards, or cash.

What exactly does "that" in the second sentence refer to? Does "that" refer to the theft or does "that" refer to the fact that Jim was careless and wasn't looking? To clear up the ambiguity, we have to be specific. The way to be specific is to add a noun after "that" to explain exactly what caused "untold problems."

> While Jim wasn't looking, someone stole his wallet. That *theft* caused him untold problems since he was stranded in a strange city without a driver's license, credit cards, or cash.

Since there's ambiguity, which is caused by an unclear demonstrative pronoun, the original sentence could also mean:

> While Jim wasn't looking, someone stole his wallet. That *carelessness* caused him untold problems since he was stranded in a strange city without a driver's license, credit cards, or cash.

In either case, exactly what caused Jim's problems has to be identified by the writer: to do so, add a noun, "theft" or "carelessness," after the demonstrative "that."

Once we've cleared up the ambiguity in the second correction, we can make the sentence even better by changing "that carelessness" to "his carelessness." But before we get to that improvement, we have to figure out what "that" refers to.

Here's one final example of the ambiguity caused by an unclear pronoun reference:

> Both Mrs. Smith and Mrs. Jones were devastated to learn that **her** son Dan was expelled from school.

In the previous sentence, we have two women, one son. Is Dan Mrs. Smith's boy or Mrs. Jones's son? We can't be certain from the way the sentence is written. The pronoun reference "her" is unclear; it could refer to either woman. Here are the ways the sentence could be reworded to make the identities of mother and son clear:

> Both Mrs. Smith and Mrs. Jones were devastated to learn that *Mrs. Smith's* son Dan was expelled from school.

> or

> Both Mrs. Smith and Mrs. Jones were devastated to learn that *Mrs. Jones's* son Dan was expelled from school.

The St. Martin's Handbook, one of the best academic handbooks for grammar, style, and research, identifies using an unclear demonstrative pronoun as one of the ten most common errors in English usage. Don't be surprised if you're asked to recognize this type of error on the SAT or to identify the best way to correct this kind of mistake.

Realizing that you aced the SAT can be quite satisfying.

LESSON 8: INCONSISTENT PRONOUN REFERENCES

Another grammatical error to look for on the SAT is the inconsistent use of a pronoun. What the term "inconsistent use of a pronoun" means is that if you start a sentence with one personal pronoun, for example, "one," don't shift to "you," in the next breath. The following sentences contain this kind of error:

> If **one** really wants to become a precise writer, **you** need to put down the cell phone and read, read, and read some more. Samuel Cohen, editor of *50 Essays: A Portable Anthology*, quotes the poet Jane Kenyon, who advises aspiring writers to "have good sentences in **your** ears." And the only way to have good sentences in **one's** ears is to read good writing.

"One" is a third-person, singular personal pronoun, while "you" is a second-person, singular personal pronoun. The pronouns don't match. They need to be consistent: third with third, or second with second. You don't have to recite that rule to be able to spot an inconsistency: "one" and in the next breath "you."

I'm not a betting person; however, I'll make a "gentleman's wager" (in a "gentleman's wager," the loser doesn't have to pay anything) that this kind of error will appear somewhere in the writing sections of the SAT. Be prepared to recognize it, and, if asked, be able to select an acceptable revision. The correction of the previous example is:

> If *you* really want to become a precise writer, *you* need to put down the cell phone and read, read, and read some more. Samuel Cohen, editor of *50 Essays: A Portable Anthology,* quotes the poet Jane Kenyon, who advises aspiring writers to "have good sentences in *your* ears." And the only way to have good sentences in *your* ears is to read good writing.

LESSON 9: FAULTY COMPARISONS

Faulty or illogical comparisons appear in academic and professional writing and show up frequently in the multiple-choice writing sections of the SAT practice tests. This kind of error involves mixing "apples and oranges," or comparing two things that may seem similar but are actually quite different. Faulty comparisons try to compare batting averages to baseball players, paintings to painters, science projects to students.

Here are several examples of faulty comparisons:

A. The **batting average of Bryce Harper** was higher than **Mickey Mantle** during Mantle's rookie season.

B. Our art history professor said that she prefers the **paintings of Cezanne** to **Renoir**.

C. The judges awarded first place to **Reema's science project** rather than to **Tariq**.

In Sentence A, a batting average is being compared to a baseball legend, Mickey Mantle. Batting averages need to be compared with batting averages and not players. The correction reads:

The batting average of Bryce Harper was higher than *that of* Mickey Mantle during Mantle's rookie season.

or

The batting average of Bryce Harper was higher than the *batting average of* Mickey Mantle during Mantle's rookie season.

In Sentence B, paintings are being compared to a painter. Paintings need to be compared with paintings, not artists. Here's the correction:

Our art history professor said that she prefers the paintings of Cezanne to *those of* Renoir.

or

Our art history professor said that she prefers the paintings of Cezanne to *the paintings of* Renoir.

In Sentence C, a first-place award is being compared to a student. A science project needs to be compared with the science project of another contestant, not the contestant himself or herself. The correction reads:

The judges awarded first place to Reema's science project rather than to *that of* Tariq.

or

The judges awarded first place to Reema's science project rather than to *the project of* Tariq.

Most faulty comparisons that you'll see on the SAT will be of the "apples and oranges" variety; however, there are also several other faulty comparisons to be aware of. Remember that officially the SAT is a test of your verbal and math skills; unofficially, it's a marathon that will test your endurance and concentration. For nearly four hours, you will have to solve math problems and demonstrate your verbal aptitude including your writing and editing skills. It's not surprising that because of the length of the test, you can easily read right past a mistake and fail to identify some of the most obvious grammatical errors that you would automatically catch under normal, non-test conditions.

For instance, no one has to explain to you the grammatical rule about the proper use of comparative and superlative adjectives and adverbs. You know, without being reminded, that when two people, two places, or two things are being compared you use the comparative form of the adjective, for example, "brighter" or "more elegant" or "less studious."[1]

You already know all of this, but when you're tired, and it becomes difficult to concentrate in the waning minutes of the SAT, an easy error might just slip past you, such as, "between Laurence Sterne and Tobias Smollett, Sterne is the **most complex** to read." Only *two* 18th-century British authors are being compared, so we have to use the comparative degree of comparison—"more complex," not the superlative—"most complex." The correct version of the comparison is:

> Between Laurence Sterne and Tobias Smollett, Sterne is the *more* complex.

---

[1] When we compare two people, two objects, two places, and so on, we use the comparative form of the adjective. For **one-syllable adjectives**, we add "r" or "er" to the end of the adjective, for example, "tall" + *er* to form *taller*, as in "Sam is *taller* than his brother Tom," or "wise" + "r" to form *wiser*, as in "he is *wiser* today than he was yesterday." For **adjectives with two or more syllables**, like "meticulous" or "diligent," we put "more" before the adjective. "She is *more meticulous* than…" "Of the two brothers, he is the *more diligent*." We would never say or write, "meticulouser" or "diligenter," nor would we say, "more taller." We just know that those constructions are wrong. The same logic applies to the superlative degree of adjectives: when **three or more** people, places, things, etc., are being compared, we add the ending "-est" to a **one-syllable adjective**, as in "tall" + "est," to form *tallest,* as in "Jack is the *tallest* boy in his class." With adjectives of **two or more syllables**, we put "most" before the word, as in "She is the *most meticulous* person I know." So don't let an error like that one slip past you on the test: "Rachel is *more quicker* than her sister." (I've seen one or two errors like that one on the SAT practice tests, and you need to be alert to catch any of those kinds of mistakes, especially toward the end of the test.)

If you were to read, "of Henry Fielding, Tobias Smollett, and Laurence Sterne, Sterne is the **more complex**," then the sentence would be wrong. The correct comparison is:

> Of Henry Fielding, Tobias Smollett, and Laurence Sterne, Sterne is the *most* complex.

Three British authors are being compared in terms of their complexity, and the other two can't match Sterne's, so "most complex" is the correct form.

So be alert as you approach the SAT's finish line for the most obvious errors that time and fatigue may obscure. "Stay the course," so that you can catch something as egregious (have you looked up that word yet?) as, "more brighter" or "most tallest." Don't be fooled for a second.

There is one more type of faulty comparison that we should look at before turning our attention to the "2-is-not-1" error. Consider the following sentence:

> The Washington Monument is taller than **any** structure in downtown Washington.

What makes this sentence incorrect is that the Washington Monument is a structure in downtown Washington, yet the sentence says that the monument is taller than any structure there. In other words, as the sentence reads, the Washington Monument is taller than itself. Impossible. The correction of this illogical comparison is:

> The Washington Monument is taller than any *other* structure in downtown Washington.

LESSON 10: THE 2-IS-NOT-1 ERROR

One common error in writing, which is a good candidate for one of the SAT's writing sections, is what I call the "2-is-not-1" error. While the logic of the title seems to be clear, its meaning may need some explanation by way of examples. You will probably see something like this sentence on the test:

> More than **one hundred applicants** submitted their **resumé** to be considered for the vacancy in the English Department.

At first glance, the sentence appears to be fine. That's actually how many would say or write the sentence, and we wouldn't give it another thought; however, the grammar of that sentence is incorrect, so let's look at the sentence a bit more closely. There were one hundred applicants for the job, yet the sentence mentions only one resumé. More than one hundred applicants, one resumé… the numbers don't add up, and something is obviously off. Different applicants don't share the same education or work experience, nor do they confer and submit one application. Each of the more than one hundred applicants submitted his or her own resumé reflecting a unique background, name, skill set, etc. To correct the error, we have to change "resumé" to its plural form—"resumés." The following is the correct version of the sentence:

More than one hundred applicants submitted their *resumés* to be considered for the vacancy in the English Department.

Here's another example of the "2-is-not-1" error:

After medical school, Iris and Wynona plan to become a cardiologist.

Two medical students, one position…again the numbers don't agree. The obvious correction of the error is:

After medical school, Iris and Wynona plan to become *cardiologists*.

One might object that Iris and Wynona will be part of one profession and insist that "cardiologist" is acceptable. But the field of medicine is "cardiology," which has many practitioners. The practitioners within this profession are "cardiologists." So, after a booth review, the call on the field stands: "cardiologists" is correct.

LESSON 11: MISTAKES WITH ADVERBS AND ADJECTIVES

In that unforgettable leadoff—Lesson 1: Misplaced Modifiers—I reminded you that modifiers are words, phrases, or clauses that give information about other words. I think that we all came away from that lesson with an even stronger conviction that *Relax I* is a "keeper" and that where a writer places a modifier in the sentence is essential to get across his or her meaning. Conversely, a writer who places a modifier haphazardly can elicit some unintentional laughs. (Don't forget Ms. Shandy, a colony of insects, and the African anteater.)

Adjectives and adverbs are clearly modifiers. An adjective gives information about a noun or a pronoun.

> Tran wore an *elegant* dress last night.

The adjective "elegant" is an adjective that modifies or gives information about Tran's dress, namely that it was lovely and chic.

An adverb gives information, most often about an action, for instance:

> Tara walked *slowly* onto the dance floor.

The adverb "slowly" tells us something about how Tara walked, namely her speed or rather the deliberate lack of it. In this latter case, "slowly" modifies a verb. Sometimes, however, an adverb can modify an adjective, for example:

Kim was *uncharacteristically* quiet at the wedding.

The adverb tells us something about Kim's behavior, namely, that it was not typical. The writer's not necessarily saying that Kim is a chatterbox, but the sentence means that she usually holds her own in a conversation, but, in this situation, she was quiet.

Don't be surprised if the SAT contains one or two sentences that contain mistakes involving adverbs and adjectives. Let's look at Kim again. Imagine a sentence on the SAT that reads:

Kim was **uncharacteristic** quiet at the wedding.

You would know that the sentence is incorrect. First of all, it just doesn't sound correct, but the "school-book" reason that "uncharacteristic quiet" is an error is that adjectives modify nouns —not other adjectives—whereas adverbs can modify adjectives. So the correct way of describing Kim's behavior at the event is:

Kim was *uncharacteristically* quiet at the wedding.

There's another possible error on the SAT that you may be expected to recognize: the misuse of an adverb for an adjective. Verbs involving the five senses—*look, appear, sound, feel, taste,* or *smell*—are also linking verbs and therefore are followed by adjectives, not adverbs. For example, you would never say this about your date for homecoming, "he looked **handsomely**." You would say instead, "he looked *handsome*." We say, "it really smelled *bad*." We don't say, "it really smelled **badly**."

Compare these sentences:

Her hands felt **smoothly**. (No)
Her hands felt *smooth*. (Yes)

She looked **beautifully**. (No)
She looked *beautiful*. (Yes)

It sounded **horribly**. (No)
It sounded *horrible*. (No)

The fish sauce smelled **badly**. (No)
The fish sauce smelled *bad*. (Yes)

The fruit tasted **sweetly**. (No)
The fruit tasted *sweet*. (Yes)

Jack Armbruster's voice sounded **weakly**. (No)
Jack Armbruster's voice sounded *weak*. (Yes)

So with adjectives and adverbs test your ear or your grammatical intuition. If something doesn't sound correct, it may be an error, and double-check that feeling with your knowledge that adjectives modify nouns and pronouns, while adverbs modify verbs, adjectives, and even other adverbs, for example:

Henry is walking *so* slowly.

Try to write an SAT practice essay at least once a week.
Limit yourself to 25 minutes—
the time limit that you'll face on the exam.

LESSON 12: "WHO" VS. "WHOM"

We were reviewing relative pronouns one day in class, when P.J. asked, "how do you know when to use 'who' and when to use 'whom'?" It was a great question. As I was gathering my thoughts, Pilar Brown, another one of my favorites, jumped in and passed on how her teacher in middle school had explained the difference to her. (I would happily give full credit to that teacher for offering such a clear explanation, but I haven't been able to track Pilar down for the source. Stay tuned. Perhaps, in the next edition, I'll be able to give that teacher the credit she deserves.)

The explanation of Pilar's teacher went something like this: If you don't know whether to use "who" or "whom," look at the antecedent—the noun that "who" or "whom" refers to. If the antecedent is singular, substitute *he* or *she* for "who" and *him* or *her* for "whom." If the antecedent is plural, substitute *they* for "who" or *them* for "whom." Read the sentence with the substitution, and, if it sounds o.k., then you have the correct relative pronoun—*who* or *whom*. If it sounds weird, then you know you have to choose the other option.

Let's apply Pilar's rule of thumb to a couple of examples:

A. I asked the author whom I believe has written several other novels how she gets her inspiration.

B. The recently retired players who I think we should consider for the NFL's Hall of Fame are Ray Lewis and Brett Favre.

Sentence A doesn't sound bad as it's written, especially since it seems as if "whom" would be the object of "I believe." Now substitute *her* for "whom" and restate the sentence:

...I believe **her** has written several other novels...

That substitution is obviously wrong. It should read:

...I believe *she* has written several other novels...

That sounds fine. We're not quite finished. Since "her" and its counterpart "whom" are incorrect, we must choose the other option: "who." We now have the correct relative pronoun to be put back into the sentence. The correct version of Sentence A is:

I asked the author *who* I believe has written several other novels how she gets her inspiration. (Yes)

We'll use Pilar's rule of thumb again and apply it to Sentence B. First, we substitute *they* for "who," since there are two great players mentioned in the sentence—Ray Lewis and Brett Favre. Then restate the sentence. The restated sentence reads,

...I think we should consider **they** for the NFL's Hall of Fame...

Obviously, the option "they" is incorrect. So let's see how *them* sounds in the sentence:

...I think we should consider *them* for the NFL's Hall of Fame...

Insert the correct relative pronoun—*whom*—for "them" and the sentence is now correct:

The recently retired players *whom* I think we should consider for the NFL's Hall of Fame are Ray Lewis and Brett Favre. (Yes)

LESSON 13: ERRORS WITH VERB TENSES

Tense is how I feel when an old college friend shows up unannounced and wants to stay at our place "just for a couple of days." Tense is how I feel when traffic's at a standstill on Constitution Avenue, and I'm already late for a meeting in Washington, D.C. Tense may be how you feel when you hear the terms, "early admissions," "financial aid," "SAT preparation," or "college admissions essay."

Another kind of tense has nothing at all to do with annoyance or stress, and everything to do with verbs. A verb tense—present, past, future—lets the reader or listener know the time of an action or a condition. Most of the time, verb tenses don't give us any problems: we can rely, as I mentioned in Lesson 6, on our "competence grammar," that tells us that something's way off when we read or hear a badly mangled sentence in our native language. Do we really have to discuss sentences like these: "John borrowed the novel from he girlfriend, Cassandra," or, as my Army drill instructor Sergeant Warren once eloquently demanded, "Sullivan, polish them boot"? We don't need English teachers to tell us that these sentences are horrible. There are, however, several English verb tenses that tend to give us problems, and these tenses are candidates to appear on the SAT.

Present perfect

When we *perfect* an action, we complete it; the *present*, of course, relates to the here and now. So the *present perfect tense* is used when an action has been completed, AND the action has a

45

connection with the *present moment*. For instance, we use the tense in this way:

> During the last fifty years, the telecommunications industry *has developed* many innovative devices.

The development has been completed between the 1960s and the present moment. We could even mentally add the phrase "up until now" at the end of the sentence, and the meaning would be even clearer. What's also understood is that more innovative devices will be developed.

Here's another example. The sentence, "her plane has finally arrived," conveys the ideas that an action has been completed ("arrived"), yet the action also relates to the present moment ("*now* our wait is over" or "*now* we can see her" or "*now* we only have to pay for two hours of parking" or "*now* we have to hear her rave again about *Relax I*").

Simple Past

We use the simple past tense to convey the idea that an action is finished. It's over and done with. It's history. "I *went* to the gym *yesterday* morning." The action of going to the gym is finished, and while the workout may have some benefits that I'm feeling now, yesterday's workout is done.

Here's a comparison of the simple past tense with the present perfect tense:

Simple Past:

Past	Present
In 1983, I bought one of the first mobile phones.	X

[The action's complete. It's history. It's toast. The action doesn't occur over a period of time. It's "one and done." There's no connection to the present.]

Present Perfect:

<u>Past</u>   <u>Present</u>
Since 1983, many innovative
telecommunications devices
have been developed.   ⟶   UP UNTIL NOW

[The action's *perfected*. It's been completed over a period of time, between 1983 and the present. If you were to mentally add the phrase "up until now," the sense of the present perfect tense would become even clearer. It's understood that more innovations will follow.]

You may be asking yourself, "why on earth is he getting into all this?" The reason's simple: on at least four occasions the SAT practice tests have included errors with these tenses, so there's a fairly good chance that you'll be expected to recognize them on the test itself. If you were to say or write, "I never ate raw oysters in my life," I would commend you for your dietary decisions, but I'd fault you for your misuse of verb tenses. The correction of course is, "I've never eaten raw oysters in my life." Good diet. Good grammar.

If a second reaction of yours to this discussion is "he's really being picky," remember what you're trying to accomplish: to prepare for the SAT. Most people wouldn't worry about the distinctions between the simple past and the present perfect tenses. The SAT test-makers, however, aren't "most people." They design tests to separate the above-average or exceptional reader and writer from the average or typical one so that colleges and universities can gauge a student's readiness for college.

Read over these final examples to reinforce or to gain mastery of the grammatical patterns of the simple past and the present perfect tenses:

> I *have never eaten* raw oysters in my life.
> [Mentally add, "up to and including this moment," and the correct verb form is clear.]

> I *didn't eat* raw oysters last night.
> [Last night is gone, and so is last night's chance to eat raw oysters.]

> Since last June, Devon *has read* seventeen novels.
> [Mentally add "up till now." The sense is clear, and the verb form is correct. Also, it's very unlikely that she'll stop reading novels.]

> Gavin *read Tom Jones* last summer.
> [That activity is over and done with, so the use of the simple past tense is correct.]

> We *have* finally *completed* our income taxes.
> [The action has been at last completed, and now there's a certain relief that what may have taken some time and effort has been completed.]

> Our next-door neighbors *completed* their taxes last week.
> [The action is over and done with.]

Past Perfect

When two actions happened in the past and we want to show that one of those actions occurred before the other one, we use the past perfect, for example:

> She *had already left*, by the time her boyfriend arrived.

In this example, there are two actions—"leaving" and "arriving." Both happened in the past; however, the girl's departure happened before the boyfriend's arrival. In order to make that distinction clear, we use the past perfect for the earlier action, "had left," and the simple past for the later one, "arrived." Most people when they hear or read, "she left before her boyfriend arrived," wouldn't give it a second thought. That kind of reaction is typical, and, as I mentioned in the previous section, since the SAT is designed to identify varying skill levels of high school students, don't be surprised if you see something like that previous example on the test. Remember that the average total score that students earn on the SAT is about 1,500 or about 500 points for each section (math, writing, and reading). You already know that the average or typical reader probably won't catch the errors with the past perfect or the present perfect tenses. You, however, will do better. Here's another example of the correct use of the past perfect:

> I *had finished* the exam just before the proctor told us to stop writing.

Future Perfect

When we can project into the future and identify that an action will be over by a certain time, we use the future perfect. For example, let's imagine that a good friend of yours invites you to go with her and her family to Ocean City, Maryland, during the first week of June. Then she remembers that you will be graduating at about that time. The future perfect tense comes to your rescue, however, when you point out that graduation will be in late May. Here's the conversation in its entirety:

> **Your Friend**: My family and I would like to invite you to go to Ocean City with us in the first week of June, but that's the week of your graduation.

> **You**: Actually, I *will have already graduated* by then. Graduation will be in late May.

If the typical reader or listener were to hear, "I will already graduate by then," he or she would be perfectly comfortable with the expression, but again, for the purposes of preparing for the SAT's writing sections, you don't want to be just the typical or average reader. You want to be able to assume the role of a careful editor and catch the errors that most people overlook in their writing or speaking. That editorial sense is exactly what we're trying to sharpen with *Relax I* so that you will separate yourself from the average reader and score higher on the SAT.

Simple Present

We use the simple present (I *drink*, you *drink*, she *drinks*, he *drinks*, it *drinks*, we *drink*, they *drink*) to express habits, routines, or recurrences in nature. For example, "my uncle drinks two cups of coffee every morning," "water freezes at 32 degrees Fahrenheit," "my sister goes to the gym every other day" are all proper uses of the simple present. We would never write "my uncle is drinking two cups of coffee every day," nor would we write, "water is freezing at 32 degrees Fahrenheit." If we need to make the point that an action is occurring at the time of speaking or writing, we would use the present continuous, but we would express it this way, "the water is boiling now." We would use "the water"—not just "water" because we're talking about a specific pot or beaker of water—not water in general. We also wouldn't be interested in the temperature at which a particular pot of water is boiling because that fact is already established.

Compare the two different meanings and the different verb tenses:

Water *freezes* at 32 degrees Fahrenheit.
[Every recorded time]

The water *is boiling*.
[At the moment of speaking or writing]

So we use the simple present when we're talking about habits, routines, and recurring events in nature. Let's now look more closely at the form and uses of the present continuous tense.

Present Continuous

We use the present continuous to describe actions going on at this very moment, for example, "you are reading this book," but we also use the present continuous tense to refer to actions occurring close to the time of speaking or writing.

As a review, here is a conjugation of the present continuous tense: I *am reading,* you *are watching,* she *is listening* to Bach, it *is eating* from its bowl, he *is taking* Calculus I, we *are learning* Spanish, they *are attending* St. Mary's High School.

Imagine this situation: last week your teacher assigned Mark Twain's *Adventures of Huckleberry Finn.* You've started the novel, you're about one third of the way into the book, and, for the time being, you've put it aside. To express that situation, write or say:

I *am reading Adventures of Huckleberry Finn.*

Would you be reading at the very moment of speaking? No, because you've put the book aside for the time being, but you would be in the middle of an action that you will resume soon and that will take some time. (You would not say or write, "I read *Adventures of Huckleberry Finn."* That tense is the simple present, which is reserved, as we mentioned before, for expressing habits.)

Here's another example of the present continuous tense: you have a friend whose parents have enrolled him in an SAT preparation course that will last a month; the first class has already met. We would say or write:

Carmelo *is taking* an SAT preparation course.

(Our thoughts and prayers go out to you, Carmelo.) Carmelo may not be attending the course at the very moment that you're speaking or writing, but he is in the middle of an activity that will be going on for a while with many other things interrupting his SAT course and actually taking much more time.

There's one final point about the present continuous tense that I need to mention. As a rule, we do not use the present continuous tense with the following verbs that deal with the "heart" or the "head," unless we're trying to be funny: *like, dislike, love, hate, know, think, believe, want, need, prefer, realize, hear, see, remember, forget, seem, suppose, understand, mean, belong.*

We would say or write:	We would NOT say or write:
I *like* the novel.	I **am liking** the novel.
She *dislikes* American football.	She **is disliking** American football.
We *want* to learn French.	We **are wanting** to learn French.
That copy of *Relax I* *belongs* to me.	That copy of *Relax I* **is belonging** to me.
Carmelo's parents *don't understand* him.	Carmelo's parents **are not understanding** him.

The Other Continuous Tenses

Think of all the continuous tenses—present, past, and future—as the tenses that really convey the idea that a person or thing is "in the middle of something" or hasn't yet finished it, AND that the activity may or may not be happening at the very moment of speaking or writing. To try to reinforce this notion that the continuous tenses really mean "in the middle of an action," let's look briefly at the past and future continuous tenses.

Here's a scenario that applies to the past continuous tense: last night, you started reading *Adventures of Huckleberry Finn*. You had gotten two chapters into the book and had just started the third chapter when your friend Carmelo called to tell you that he hates his SAT preparation course and how lucky you are to be preparing for it on your own…with *Relax I*. Describe this situation with the past continuous:

> I *was reading* a novel last night when Carmelo called.

You were in the middle of an action, in the past, when something else occurred.

The future continuous is used to refer to a situation and action that you can project into the future but will not be finished at that moment in time. To illustrate this point, let's assume that you have to work tomorrow night. As a result, you can't go to a concert with your friends, so you express the thought this way:

> Think of me while you're at the concert. I *will be cleaning* the floors.

Inconsistent Verb Tenses

Another frequent writing error that appears on the SAT practice tests and may appear on the SAT itself is the use of different verb tenses for actions that occur at the same time. For example, you might see a sentence like:

> Throughout his adult life, Laurence Sterne, the 18th-century British novelist, **suffered** from a lung disease; nonetheless, he **writes** several hours every day of his life.

Since the sentence tells us that Sterne lived in the 18th century, the time of the two actions, "the suffering" and "the writing" should both be past tense. The original sentence offers different tenses for the same timeframe, which, in any situation, is clearly wrong. The correction of course reads:

> Throughout his adult life, Laurence Sterne, the 18th-century British novelist, *suffered* from a lung disease; nonetheless, he *wrote* several hours every day of his life.

Let's examine one more example of inconsistent verb tenses, and then we'll move on:

> The three weird sisters **prophesy** that Macbeth will be king; almost immediately, Macbeth **started to have** dark ambitions about becoming king.

The "prophesying" and the "having ambition" occur at the same time in the play, but the verb tenses in the previous sentence don't match—one's present and one's past. Here's the correction:

> The three weird sisters *prophesy* that Macbeth will be king; almost immediately, Macbeth *starts to have* dark ambitions about becoming king.

Free of charge: When you're narrating material from a source in literature or scholarship, use the present tense, which is called "the historical present tense," for example, "Huck Finn *lies* to the bounty-hunters about Jim, then Huck *feels* conscience-stricken," "Aristotle in *The Rhetoric identifies* the ethos of the speaker as a primary means of persuasion," and "The Declaration of Independence *affirms* the right of people to break free from any form of government that violates their innate rights."

LESSON 14: LACK OF AGREEMENT OF A VERB WITH ITS SUBJECT

The lack of agreement of verbs with their subjects ranks as public enemy number one among common grammatical errors in English. I've placed our discussion of this type of error here in *Relax I* because earlier I reviewed in passing some of the terms that make this lesson a little easier to follow. This error crops up so frequently in high school, college, and professional writing that you can be confident that it will appear at least once, perhaps more often, on the multiple-choice writing sections of the SAT. The lack of agreement of a verb with its subject may creep into your own papers as well, so it's important to be able to spot lack of agreement errors and to correct them, or better yet, to avoid them altogether in your own writing.

All right, it's confession time. As I was drafting this part of *Relax I*, I was somewhat at a loss on how to proceed. To explain how to make verbs agree with (that is, "match") their subjects, I knew that I would need to explain the concepts of "person" and "number." Many of you, however, were fortunate enough to have had a solid grounding in grammatical terms in elementary school or middle school or both, so an extensive review would be unnecessary and might even be an annoyance, creating a reason for you not to continue. Other readers, however, may not have had the same training and need to understand the terms of "person" and "number" to master the rules for correctly matching verbs with their subjects.

My dilemma, then, as a writer and teacher was: do I risk losing half my readers by going over material that they don't need, or do I omit an explanation of these important terms and possibly lose the other half of my audience? After struggling with this dilemma for a while, I decided to do the "brave" thing and do nothing at all: I'm going to leave it up to you. If you're fortunate enough to have a solid grounding in grammar, then scan the explanatory material on "person" and "number" that immediately follows. If it's material that you don't need and that you have "down cold," go straight to "Seven Types of Lack of Agreement of Verb with Subject Errors." The only thing that I ask is that you be honest with yourself. If, after scanning the following material, "Number and Person," you have any doubts, then work your way through the explanations until you have them down. As a reality check, I encourage every one of you to complete the self-assessment after we've finished Lesson 18. That assessment will help you decide what material in *Relax I* you've mastered and what material you'll need to review.

Number and Person

The grammatical concept of "number" is simple enough: we use the term "singular" to refer to *one* person, place or thing, and the term "plural" to refer to *more than one* person, place, or thing. The grammatical concept of "person," however, is more involved.

When we refer to "person" in grammar, we are actually referring to three possibilities:

1. the term *first person* ("I" and "we") refers to the speaker or writer, sometimes called "the voice,"

2. the term *second person* ("you") refers to the audience or the reader, and

3. the term *third person* ("he," "she," or "they") refers to what or whom is being mentioned by the writer or speaker.

The following table gives the complete picture of grammar's "persons," their roles, their numbers, their status as nouns or pronouns, and examples:

Person	Examples	Number	Pronoun	Role
First	I, me, my, mine	Singular	YES	Speaker
First	we, our, us, ours	Plural	YES	Speaker
Second	you, your, yours	Singular	YES	Audience
Second	you, your, yours	Plural	YES	Audience
Third	he, his, him, she, her, hers, it, its	Singular	YES	The One Mentioned
Third	Diosa, Carmelo, P.J., the SAT Math Section, St. Mary's Ryken High School	Singular	NO (nouns)	The Ones Mentioned
Third	they, their, them, theirs	Plural	YES	The Ones Mentioned
Third	Universities, applications, essays, scores, St. Mary's Knights, the people's choice, brown bears.	Plural	NO (nouns)	The Ones Mentioned

EXERCISE 1

Identify the person and number of the following words. Also, tell whether the word is a noun or a pronoun.

1. We: _____   _____   _____
      Person   Number   Pronoun (P) or Noun (N)

2. He: _____   _____   _____
      Person   Number   Pronoun (P) or Noun (N)

3. Plato: _____   _____   _____
      Person   Number   Pronoun (P) or Noun (N)

4. I: _____   _____   _____
      Person   Number   Pronoun (P) or Noun (N)

5. She: _____   _____   _____
      Person   Number   Pronoun (P) or Noun (N)

6. Ida: _____   _____   _____
      Person   Number   Pronoun (P) or Noun (N)

7. Forms:_____   _____   _____
      Person   Number   Pronoun (P) or Noun (N)

8. University:

      _____   _____   _____
      Person   Number   Pronoun (P) or Noun (N)

9. They: _____   _____   _____
      Person   Number   Pronoun (P) or Noun (N)

10. Jury: _____   _____   _____
      Person   Number   Pronoun (P) or Noun (N)

THE CORRECT ANSWERS for EXERCISE 1

1. We: <u>1ST</u>   <u>Plural</u>   <u>P</u>
          Person   Number   Pronoun (P) or Noun (N)

2. He: <u>3RD</u>   <u>Singular</u>   <u>P</u>
          Person   Number   Pronoun (P) or Noun (N)

3. Plato: <u>3RD</u>   <u>Singular</u>   <u>N</u>
          Person   Number   Pronoun (P) or Noun (N)

4. I: <u>1ST</u>   <u>Singular</u>   <u>P</u>
          Person   Number   Pronoun (P) or Noun (N)

5. She: <u>3RD</u>   <u>Singular</u>   <u>P</u>
          Person   Number   Pronoun (P) or Noun (N)

6. Ida: <u>3RD</u>   <u>Singular</u>   <u>N</u>
          Person   Number   Pronoun (P) or Noun (N)

7. Forms: <u>3RD</u>   <u>Plural</u>   <u>N</u>
          Person   Number   Pronoun (P) or Noun (N)

8. University:

          <u>3RD</u>   <u>Singular</u>   <u>N</u>
          Person   Number   Pronoun (P) or Noun (N)

9. They: <u>3RD</u>   <u>Plural</u>   <u>P</u>
          Person   Number   Pronoun (P) or Noun (N)

10. Jury: <u>3RD</u>   <u>Singular</u>   <u>N</u>
          Person   Number   Pronoun (P) or Noun (N)

Verbs also have "person" and "number." For example, the proper forms of the simple present for first, second, and third person— singular and plural forms of the verb "enjoy"— look like this:

> I *enjoy*. You *enjoy*. He *enjoys*. She *enjoys*. It *enjoys*. We *enjoy*. You *enjoy*. They *enjoy*.

In the simple present, all the forms of the verb are the same **except for** the third person singular. Note the ending—"s"—added to the verb for third person singular. If I were to say or write, "Carmella enjoy," it would be wrong, obviously, because there would be a **lack of agreement** of the **verb** with its **subject**. In other words, the verb does not match its subject. Look at this example:

> My cat Dara and my dog Monkey **enjoys** running in the yard.

"My cat Dara and my dog Monkey" are two pets, so the subject is plural. The verb, "enjoys," is singular. Again, there is a mismatch between the singular form "enjoys" and its plural subject "Dara and Monkey." The verb doesn't match the subject. Here's the correction:

> My cat Dara and my dog Monkey *enjoy* running in the yard.

Many of the lack of agreement problems occur when the subject is third person and the verb is simple present.

> My uncle **drink** coffee every morning. (No)
> My uncle *drinks* coffee every morning. (Yes)

> They **works** hard. (Really?)
> They *work* hard. (Yes)

> Plant life in many forms **are** thriving in the rain forest. (No)
> Plant life in many forms *is* thriving in the rain forest. (Yes)

Seven Types of Errors Involving
Lack of Agreement of Verb with Subject

We are now ready to cover in detail the seven occasions when the lack of agreement of a verb with its subject occurs:

1. When the subject follows the verb,

2. When modifiers separate the subject from the verb,

3. When the subject looks plural but is singular,

4. When the subject is part of a "neither...nor," or "either...or" construction,

5. When afterthoughts ("tagalongs") are added to the subject,

6. When collective nouns are the subject, and

7. When subjects and complements are involved.

When the Subject Follows the Verb

Keep in mind two things:

1. "there," as in "there is" or "there are" constructions, CANNOT be the subject of the verb, and

2. a prepositional phrase at the beginning of a sentence CANNOT be the verb's subject.

Look at this example:

There **is** several **alarm systems** in my home.

This sentence is obviously incorrect. The subject of the sentence is "alarm systems," which follows the verb. The subject is clearly a plural noun, "alarm systems," so the verb must match it in number, namely, "are." The corrected sentence reads:

> There *are* several *alarm systems* in my home.

Here's a second example:

> There **are** one manuscript of the author's science fiction story.

This sentence is just as bad as the first uncorrected sentence. In the second sentence, the subject, "manuscript," which is singular, follows the verb. Now we must make the verb match it, namely:

> There *is* only one manuscript of the author's science fiction story.

I haven't said anything that's groundbreaking: the errors in these two examples are obvious. There are, however, less obvious examples of errors involving the lack of agreement of a verb with its subject when the subject follows the verb. Take a look at these two sentences:

> A. Near the bottom of Lake Baikal **lies** several species of marine life just recently discovered by biologists.
>
> B. Into the highlands, ahead of the others, **run** the alpha-male gorilla.

Sentence A contains a mismatch of the verb and subject. You may recall that a prepositional phrase, such as "Near the bottom of Lake Baikal," at the beginning of a sentence CANNOT be the verb's subject. The subject, which follows the verb, is "several species." It's a plural noun, so the verb must match its plural subject. The corrected sentence reads:

> Near the bottom of Lake Baikal *lie* several species of marine life just recently discovered by biologists.

What's confusing is that immediately before the verb is a singular noun, "Lake Baikal." We might have the tendency to match a verb with what immediately comes before it. In that tendency lies the problem. So to prevent this confusion and error, find the subject of the sentence or clause and match the verb with it. Prepositional phrases are modifiers and give information, but they cannot be subjects of clauses or sentences.

Sentence B also contains an error involving the lack of agreement of the verb with its subject. Sentence B begins with two prepositional phrases, "into the highlands," and "ahead of the others." Neither one can be the sentence's subject. The subject is "the alpha-male gorilla." It's a singular noun, so the verb must agree with it and be in the singular form too, namely, "runs." The corrected sentence reads:

> Into the highlands, ahead of the others, *runs* the alpha-male gorilla.

When Modifiers Separate the Subject from the Verb

The discussion of this type of error is best introduced with an example.

> One scholar claims that **the Transcendentalists** of 19th-century New England, including Henry David Thoreau, who would later become an inspiration to Dr. Martin Luther King, Jr., **was met** with derision and contempt by some of their contemporaries.

The subject of the clause (beginning with "that") is "Transcendentalists," a plural noun, yet the verb is "was met," which is singular. Clearly, there is a mismatch in number between the subject and the verb: one is plural, the other is singular. So we have, in this example, a classic example of lack of agreement of the verb with its subject. What causes the error? One reason is that the writer has lost track of the subject and has matched the verb—not with the plural subject itself, "Transcendentalists"—but with "Dr. Martin Luther King, Jr.," a singular noun, which comes immediately before the verb. Losing track of the subject is understandable when several modifiers separate the verb from the subject. First, the phrases, "of 19th-century New England," and "including Henry David Thoreau," modify the subject, "Transcendentalists." These modifiers give information about the Transcendentalists: when (19th century) and where (New England) they came into prominence and who was one of the movement's prominent writers and thinkers (Thoreau). The third modifier, which separates the subject from the verb, is the clause, "who would later become an inspiration to Dr. Martin Luther King, Jr."

So how do we recognize this common error and eliminate it from our own writing, especially if there is a great deal of modification that separates the subject from the verb?

Follow these steps, and you won't have a problem in identifying this type of error on the SAT or in your own drafts.

1. Locate the grammatical subject of the sentence or the clause. In the example above, the grammatical subject is "Transcendentalists."

2. Locate the subject's verb, which, in this case, is "was met."

3. Don't be distracted by modifiers that separate the subject from the verb. Focus on matching the verb with the subject. In the example, the distracting modifiers are the prepositional phrases, "of 19th-century New England" and "including Henry David Thoreau," and the clause, "who would later become an inspiration to Dr. Martin Luther King, Jr." For the purposes of matching verbs with subjects, don't even consider any distracting modifiers. They're not even there.

4. Now that you've isolated the subject and the verb and
    you've removed any distractions between the subject and
    the verb, match the number of the verb with the number of
    the subject: "Transcendentalists," the subject, is plural in
    number, so the verb form must be plural as well—"were
    met."

    subject   *modifier (phrase)*
      ↓   ↓

The <u>Transcendentalists</u> [of 19th-century New England,]

    modifier (phrase)   *modifier (clause)*
         ↓   ↓

[including Henry David Thoreau] [who would later
become an inspiration to Dr. Martin Luther King, Jr.,]

verb
 ↓

<u>*were*</u> met with derision and contempt by some of their
contemporaries.

Let's look at one more example:

> **Shakespeare**, of all the Elizabethan dramatists, most of
> whom were educated at the university and called the
> "University Wits," **were** successful in business ventures in
> London and in Stratford.

Follow the same steps that we used for the sentence about the
Transcendentalists:

1. Locate the grammatical subject, which is "Shakespeare."

2. Locate the main verb—"were."

3. Focus on the subject, "Shakespeare," and the main verb,
    "were." In matching the subject with the verb, don't

consider any of the modifiers that separate "Shakespeare" from "were."

4. There is a clear mismatch between the main verb, "were," and its subject, "Shakespeare." We correct the verb by making it singular—"was."

Here is the corrected sentence with the verb and subject agreeing in number:

> *Shakespeare*, of all the Elizabethan dramatists, most of whom were educated at the university and called the "University Wits," *was* successful in business ventures in London and in Stratford.

When the Subject Looks Plural but is Singular

Certain words in English look plural but are actually singular and have to be treated as such for the purposes of subject-verb agreement. Among them are "measles," "mumps," "shingles," and "AIDS." Measles is *an* infection that produces small, red eruptions on the skin. We wouldn't say, "measles **are** an infection." Nor would we say, "AIDS **are** a deadly disease that is ravaging West Africa." The correct versions of course are: "measles *is* an infection that produces small, red eruptions on the skin," and "AIDS *is* a deadly disease that is ravaging West Africa."

Several academic subjects also seem to be plural but are actually singular. Think of *physics, statistics, economics, biometrics,* and *robotics*. Each of these (and look in any college course catalogue, and you'll find more examples) is one course or area of study and must be treated as singular. If you were to read or hear, "statistics **are** a difficult subject," your grammatical intuition would kick in, and you'd recognize the error. The correct version is obviously "statistics *is* a difficult subject."

When the Subject is Part of a "Neither...Nor" or an "Either...Or" Construction

When the subject of a sentence or clause is part of a "neither...nor" or "either...or" construction, don't worry about anything except the noun or pronoun that follows "or" or "nor." Match the verb with the latter noun or pronoun that immediately follows "nor" or "or," for instance:

> Neither John nor his parents *were impressed* with the university's suggested reading list for incoming freshmen.

We match the verb—the past tense of "to be impressed"—with the noun closer to the verb. In this case, that noun is third person plural—"parents"—so the verb must be third person plural too, namely, "were impressed." Change the sequence and the correct sentence reads:

> Neither John's parents nor John *was impressed* with the university's suggested reading list for incoming freshmen.

Here's a final example of how to match verbs properly with subjects having "neither...nor" or "either...or" constructions:

> Either George Knightly or his servants *have been leaving* food for the poor families in the parish of Donwell Abbey. (Correct)

"Servants" is closer to the verb than "Knightly" so match the verb with "servants."

> Either George Knightly's servants or Knightly himself *has been leaving* food for the poor families in the parish of Donwell Abbey. (Correct)

"Knightly himself" is closer to the verb than "servants" so match the verb with the third person singular "Knightly himself."

When Indefinite Pronouns are Subjects

The indefinite pronouns—*each, either, neither, one, no one, nobody, anyone, anybody, anything, someone, somebody, something, everyone, everybody,* and *everything*—are all singular. When they are the subjects of sentences or clauses, you probably won't have any subject-verb agreement problems. Still, let's look at the proper way to match verbs with these indefinite pronouns when they are the subjects of sentences or clauses. (Reviewing this material will help when we come to the lesson on agreement of pronouns with their antecedents.)

"Everyone" refers to a number of people and might be considered plural, but don't be fooled. Here is the correct way a clause reads when "everyone" is the subject:

Everyone *was* in attendance.

"Everyone," the subject, is singular, so the verb must agree with its subject and be singular as well.

"Everybody **are** coming to the wedding reception" just doesn't sound correct and since we can often trust our English language intuition to put us on the right track, we know that this sentence needs to be changed. The correct version, of course, is, "Everybody *is* coming to the wedding reception."

Anything *is* possible.

Everything *was* in order.

Everyone *has been* conscientious.

Nobody *is* here yet.

Anyone who *has* ever been there *knows* how beautiful it is.

When Afterthoughts or "Tagalongs" Are Added to the Subject

Sometimes, a rule in grammar seems to defy logic. The rule that we're about to discuss is one of those types. If you were to read, "Tobias Smollett, together with Laurence Sterne…" in the nanosecond before you even read the verb, you would probably expect it to be plural. After all, Tobias Smollett and Laurence Sterne are two separate writers. They seem to be part of the same subject. More than one is plural, so the verb should be plural as well. If you were to think that way, your logic would be unassailable, and I would agree with you. We'd both be wrong.

The phrases, *in addition to, in combination with, together with, as well as*, when added to the subject of a verb, DO NOT MAKE THE SUBJECT PLURAL. Why? The textbook answer is that these phrases are just that—phrases—in effect, types of modifiers, and, by themselves, they cannot act as subjects of verbs. Remember also that phrases between the grammatical subject and its verb do not change the number of the subject. The rule is counterintuitive. It goes against the grain. You could argue about the rule, we could discuss it, you could curse it and give many sensible reasons why it isn't logical—and I would be squarely in your corner—but none of that would help you get a higher SAT writing score. So, for the sake of your sanity and your serenity, simply accept the rule, and think of the following examples so that you'll recognize the correct versions of subject-verb agreement that involve afterthoughts, or "tagalongs," to the subject:

> Tobias Smollett, *together with* Laurence Sterne, *was not appreciated* until the 20th century.

> Tobias Smollett, *in addition to* Laurence Sterne, *was not appreciated* until the 20th century."

> Tobias Smollett, *as well as* Laurence Sterne, *was not appreciated* until the 20th century."

When a Collective Noun is the Subject

A collective noun refers to a group of people, places, or things. Words like *orchestra, team, squad, assembly, class, herd, university, jury, Congress, the European Union,* are all collective nouns. Each of those nouns refers to one group with multiple members, is singular, and takes a singular verb. The logic is that a collective noun refers to a group that acts as though it were a unit, as though it were one, and it must be considered singular. Hence, we would write:

> The orchestra *is performing* Bach's *Jesu, Joy of Man's Desiring*.

> The jury *has been deliberating* for hours.

> Our lacrosse team *is* the State champion.

> The assembly *was getting* restless because the guest speaker was late.

> Congress *is* in session.

> The herd *stays* alert for predators.

> The European Union *promotes* the use of a common currency.

There is of course an exception. If the group isn't acting as a unit and the members are going about their business individually, the group is no longer one, so we would say or write:

> The jury *are* in disagreement.

Yes, I know that it sounds incorrect, but here's the reason that "are" is the correct verb form in the preceding sentence. When the members of a jury are in agreement, we consider the jury to be acting as "one," as a unit or a group, so the verb is singular;

however, when the jury isn't acting in concert and everyone has his or her own separate opinion about the guilt or innocence of the defendant, then we can no longer say that the jury is acting as a unit. For the purposes of grammar, therefore, the jury is no longer singular but plural.

Many of my students looked at me skeptically when we went over this exception. To mollify everyone, I suggested the following way to circumvent (that is, get around) the awkward-sounding, "the jury are in disagreement."

Insert "members of" in front of "the jury" so your readers or listeners won't be distracted by your correctly writing something that sounds like a mistake:

The *members of* the jury *are* in disagreement.

That insertion is my suggested change for you to be grammatically correct and to maintain the confidence of your readers.

Subjects and Complements

You know what the subject of a sentence is; the other term we're using for this discussion is "complement," which is a word or phrase that follows a linking verb and gives information about the subject. Complements can be adjectives, as in the sentence, "she is *generous.*" Complements can also be nouns, as in this sentence, "Thomas Jefferson was *President of the United States* from 1801 to 1809." For the purpose of matching subjects with verbs, we are only concerned when the complement is a noun. The rule for the correct subject-verb matchup is: **make the verb agree with the subject of the sentence and not the complement**. Here is how the rule is applied to two different sentences with identical meanings:

subject	*verb*		*complement*
↓	↓		↓

The Leonardtown Flyers are my favorite *semi-pro football team.*

subject   verb   complement
↓   ↓   ↓

My favorite *semi-pro football team is* the *Leonardtown Flyers*.

Here are two final examples:

Roses are her delight.

Her delight *is* roses.

When Compounds are Subjects

The New Oxford American Dictionary tells us that a compound "is made up of two or more existing parts or elements." Compounds, such as *France and Germany*, *quinoa and rice*, or *Thomas Hardy and Emily Bronte*, are considered plural. As a result, a compound subject requires a plural verb.

Thomas Hardy and Emily Bronte, two 19th-century novelists, *are* famous for their use of the landscape as an integral part of their novels.

France and Germany, now allies, *were* once enemies.

Quinoa and flax, staples of a plant-based diet, *are* gaining popularity among health-conscious consumers.

There is an exception, however. (So what else is new in English grammar?) When two or more people, places, or things are combined to form a unit, for the purposes of grammar, they become singular. For instance, if two lawyers, Bernstein and O'Hara, were to form a law firm, we write:

Bernstein and O'Hara, a fledgling law firm, *takes* on cases that other attorneys refuse to accept.

We consider "Bernstein and O'Hara" to be one law firm. It's the name of a firm, and therefore it's singular for the purposes of matching a verb with its subject. We would also consider the nation, Bosnia and Herzegovina, to be singular since it's one country, but with two parts to its name. Look at how sentences should be written when two or more elements are joined to form one thing—a company, a country, a food dish, and so on. In each of these cases, the unit is considered singular:

> *Bernstein and O'Hara*, a fledgling law firm, *takes* on cases that other attorneys refuse to accept.
> [It's one law firm, so it takes the singular form of the verb.]

> *Bosnia and Herzegovina*, once a republic of Yugoslavia, *is* now an independent country.
> [It's one country, so it takes the singular form of the verb.]

> *Rice and beans is* a favorite dish of my neighbors.
> [It's one dish, so it takes the singular form of the verb.]

Study by yourself. Study with a partner.
Choose the approach that better suits your learning style.

LESSON 15: LACK OF AGREEMENT OF A PRONOUN WITH ITS ANTECEDENT

A quick review of the meanings of "antecedent" and "pronoun" will set the stage for us to review a grammatical error made far too often both in casual and formal writing: lack of agreement of a pronoun with its antecedent. Our English word, "antecedent" comes from a combination of two Latin words: *ante* which means "before" and *cedent* which comes from the Latin verb *cedere* meaning "to go." Hence, an antecedent is a word that goes before something else. That something else of course is a pronoun, which takes the antecedent's place in the sentence. In the following sentences, "Zach Angel" is the antecedent, and "he" is the pronoun taking the place of "Zach Angel."

> In 2007, *Zach Angel* was voted the most valuable high school lacrosse player in the Washington Catholic Athletic Conference (WCAC). *He* was the leading scorer in the conference that year, and *he* led St. Mary's Ryken to victory in the WCAC championship game.

A number of situations involving the agreement of pronouns with their antecedents require some attention.

When Indefinite Pronouns Are Antecedents

Sometimes, indefinite pronouns can act as antecedents to other pronouns. These indefinite pronouns are singular: *each, either, neither, one, no one, nobody, anyone, anybody, anything, someone, somebody, something, everyone, everybody,* and *everything*. The plural indefinite pronouns are: *several, few, both,* and *many*. There are even indefinite pronouns that can be either singular or plural: *some, any, none, all,* or *most*. Most of the time there won't be any hesitation about correctly matching pronouns with their indefinite antecedents, for instance:

> *Each* of those pit bulls has had all *its* shots.

> *Everything* is in *its* place.

> *Anything* may be of value if *it's* given with sincerity.

> *Everyone* did *his* or *her* own thing.

Or

> *Several* took *their* time finishing the test.

> *Few* ever stop to think that *their* behavior affects other people.

> *Both* practiced *their* crafts so diligently that they became renowned short story writers.

> *Many* fail to complete or even start *their* assignments.

Some indefinite pronouns can be either singular or plural, for example, *some, any, none, all,* and *most*. When these indefinites act as antecedents, we have to make choices about whether the pronoun that follows should be singular or plural. Often, that choice can be made from the context of the sentence. In other situations, we have to determine whether the phrase that follows the indefinite pronoun contains a *count* or a *noncount* noun.

In English, a "count" noun refers to something that can be measured or, as the term suggests, counted, like ten gallons of gasoline. We can put a number on "gallons," which is a count noun, but we cannot count gasoline, which is noncount. For instance, we would never say, "I'll buy ten gasolines" since we cannot count "gasoline." We can count the units that measure or quantify it, like "gallons" in the U.S. or "liters" in other countries. So, I might put *ten gallons* of gas in my car or buy *five quarts* of oil, read *seven novels* assigned to me, resell *fourteen textbooks*, go on a trip with *three family members*, and so on.

Other nouns refer to abstractions, like *wisdom, morality, intelligence, beauty*, or substances, like *oil, gasoline, milk, sand, sugar, salt*, and so on, which we can't count or assign a number to. These nouns, obviously, are called "noncount" nouns. We can count books that express great wisdom, for instance, "there are *five philosophy books* on the table," but we can never count "wisdom," an abstraction. We would never say, "There are **five wisdoms** on the table." We might write or say, "there are *five examples* of great wisdom in the books on the table," because we can count examples or books, but never wisdom. So look at the phrase that follows one of these indefinites—*some, any, none, all*, or *most*. If the noun in that phrase is a noncount noun, then the pronoun referring to it must be singular, for instance:

> *Some* of the *gasoline* leaked from *its* container.
> ["Gasoline" is a noncount noun, so, in its role as antecedent, it takes a singular pronoun, "its."]

On the other hand, if the noun in the phrase that follows *some, any, none, all*, or *most* is count, then use a plural pronoun to refer to it, for instance:

> *Some* of the *gallons* were lost when *they* leaked from *their* container.
> ["Gallons" is a count noun, so the pronouns referring to that antecedent must be plural, "they" and "their."]

> *None* of that *sugar* should be used because pesticide contaminated *it*.
> ["Sugar" is a noncount noun so a pronoun referring to

it has to be singular—"it."]

I don't think that you should use *any* of those *containers* because *they* aren't very strong.

You can also supply other examples of these indefinites that can take either singular or plural pronouns, such as, "*none* of the *milk* has gone bad since we refrigerated *it* as soon as we came home from the store," or "*none* of the *students* did *their* homework."

When the Antecedent is Part of a "Neither...Nor" or "Either...Or" Construction

We discussed the agreement of the verb with its subject when the subject is part of a "neither...nor," or "either...or" construction. We pointed out that, for those constructions, the verb agrees with the noun that is CLOSER to the verb, for instance,

> Neither Mr. and Mrs. Hardy nor *Tom is* going to the game.

"Tom," a singular noun, is closer to the verb so we match the verb with "Tom" and not "Mr. and Mrs. Hardy." If we reverse the order, the same rule applies with a different outcome,

> Neither Tom nor *Mr. and Mrs. Hardy are* going to the game.

The same logic applies to the agreement of a pronoun with its antecedent when the antecedent is part of a "neither...nor" or "either...or" construction. In that case, we match the number (singular or plural) of the pronoun with that part of the antecedent that is CLOSER to the pronoun, for instance:

A. Neither Mr. and Mrs. Hardy nor *Tom* bought *his* ticket for the game.

B. Neither Tom nor *Mr. and Mrs. Hardy* bought *their* tickets for the game.

In Sentence A, "Tom," a singular noun and part of a "neither… nor" construction, is closer to the pronoun, so the pronoun must be singular as well—"his." "His" therefore is the correct matchup for "Tom." In Sentence B, "Mr. and Mrs. Hardy," a plural noun and part of a "neither…nor" construction, is closer to the pronoun, so the pronoun must be plural too.

When Collective Nouns are Antecedents

Most of the time, the lack of agreement of pronouns with their antecedents occurs when writers mention a collective noun, which is **singular**, such as an organization or an institution, yet use a **plural** pronoun to take its place:

> **The U.S. Geological Survey** was established in 1879. **They** are responsible for measuring seismic activity worldwide.

"The U.S. Geological Survey" refers to an organization. It, like "team," is a collective noun, which is singular. Since the antecedent is singular, its pronoun must be singular as well. Hence, the correct version of the sentence is:

> *The U.S. Geological Survey* was established in 1879. *It* is responsible for measuring seismic activity worldwide.

When Compounds are the Antecedents

Compounds, such as, "Thomas Hardy and Charlotte Bronte," consisting of more than one person, are obviously plural and take plural pronouns:

> *Thomas Hardy and Charlotte Bronte* are 19th-century British novelists renowned for *their* innovations with setting.

There's no need for a great deal of discussion on this point. Be mindful, however, that when an organization is titled with two names, it's still considered to be one group and is therefore singular. The pronoun referring to that organization must be singular as well. The reasoning is that if two attorneys form a law firm, that firm is actually one business, regardless of the two names that are used for its title. The business is singular, and any pronoun reference to that business is singular as well. Examples follow:

> *Kane and Schrider*, a law firm that got *its* start by handling personal-injury cases, has *its* main office in Virginia.
> [There are two owners but one firm, so any pronoun referring to the firm is singular.]

> *Lord and Taylor* is having *its* annual sale with all men's sportswear reduced by 10%.
> [One department store is one department store even though the store has two names in its title. As an antecedent, then, "Lord and Taylor" is singular and takes a singular pronoun—"its."]

> *Washington and Lee* offers *its* students a three-term academic year.
> [The university is titled "Washington and Lee," but it is one university and therefore singular, and the pronoun "its" is correct.]

Finally, works of literature or drama sometimes have plural titles, such as, *Adventures of Huckleberry Finn*. The title of that classic is the title of one work of literature, and should be considered to be singular. Here are examples of the correct way to match pronouns when their antecedents are plural book titles:

> Twain's *Adventures of Huckleberry Finn* is a masterpiece of irony and social commentary, and *its* value seems to increase with time.

> Chaucer's *Canterbury Tales* was written in the late 14th century. *It* opens a window onto the world of medieval England.

Professor Wagner just assigned us Dostoevsky's *The Brothers Karamazov*, but *it* must be read within two weeks.

When Antecedents are Plural in Form but Singular in Meaning

Earlier, we reviewed the point that certain words look as if they're plural but are actually singular, for example, *mumps*, *measles*, *shingles*, *AIDS*, *robotics*, *statistics*, *news*, *economics*, *physics*, etc. Remember that these nouns are singular and take singular verbs, for example, "mumps is a viral infection of the salivary glands." When nouns that are plural in form but singular in meaning are antecedents, they also take singular pronouns.

> *Mumps* is usually not dangerous, and *its* treatment often requires only bed rest and aspirin.

> *Statistics* is one of the few courses Jack enjoys. He especially likes the way *it's* presented by Dr. Wilson.

> The *news* was met with disappointment. *It* reiterated the administration's decision to raise tuition next fall.

When "a number of" or "the number of" is the Antecedent

As an antecedent, "*a* number of" should always be considered plural and take a plural pronoun, for instance, "*A number of* students left *their* IDs at home." The phrase, "*the* number of students," is considered singular both for subject-verb agreement and pronoun-antecedent agreement, for example, "*the number of* students has grown, and *it* will continue to increase during the next five years." Here are two more examples that I hope adequately reinforce the difference:

> *A number of* students decided that *they* had had enough and stood up to the class bullies—*their* tormentors—with surprising success.

Every year, for the past three years, *the number of* courses at our college has decreased, and *it* will probably continue to decrease as more teachers are fired.

When a Phrase or a Clause
Separates the Antecedent from its Pronoun

We mentioned in Lesson 14 that a phrase or a clause that separates a subject from its verb does NOT change the number of the subject. The same rule holds true for pronoun-antecedent agreement, for example:

the verb agrees with
antecedent (singular)   *the singular subject*
↓   ↓

1. Bill Thompson's *anthology* of short stories *has been*

the pronoun refers back to the
singular antecedent—"anthology"
↓

reviewed and criticized for *its* poor layout.

the verb agrees with
antecedent (plural)   *the plural subject, "poems"*
↓   ↓

2. Many of the *poems* written by Jack Armbruster *have been*

the pronoun refers back to the
plural antecedent—"poems"
↓

discovered where *their* author had originally hid *them*— in his copy of *Pilgrim's Progress*.

LESSON 16: LACK OF PARALLELISM

When you have two elements joined by a conjunction or when you have three or more elements in a series, give them the same grammatical form. In other words, make them parallel in construction. If you start with two adjectives in a series, make the third element in the series an adjective as well. If you start with two nouns in a series, make the third part of that series a noun too. Compare these two sentences:

> A. Copper is known for its ductility, conductivity, **and because it is malleable**.

> B. Copper is known for its *ductility*, *conductivity*, and *malleability*.

Version B is much better than Version A. First of all, Version B sounds better. It's also much more succinct and to the point. As a result, the writing is easier to follow, and, in the end, isn't clear communication the primary purpose of expository writing? In Sentence B, there are three nouns in a row: *ductility*, *conductivity*, and *malleability*. The sentence is nicely balanced; it's parallel in construction. In Version A, however, we have imbalance or a lack of parallelism: a noun followed by another noun, then joined with a clause. It doesn't sound very good, and one can get distracted by the shift in the sentence's structure. When I read an imbalanced construction like the one found in Sentence A, I have to go back and read the sentence again because something seems out of place. In contrast, look at how smoothly and logically the following sentence reads because of its parallel structure. (Again, I'm using unconventional spacing to present the balance that Samuel Johnson achieves in this sentence.)

> It...[is]...now...fashionable...
>
> to defame and vilify   the House of Stuart, and
> ↓   ↓   ↓   ↓   ↓   ↓   ↓   ↓
> to   exalt   and magnify the reign   of Elizabeth.

(Samuel Johnson, *Gentleman's Magazine* 1760, quoted by James Boswell in his *Life of Johnson*.)

In Samuel Johnson's sentence, the infinitives "to defame and vilify" are balanced with two other infinitives, "to exalt and magnify." The objects of these infinitive phrases are nicely balanced too—"the House of Stuart" and "the reign of Elizabeth." The parallelism creates writing that's not only pleasant to read but also easy to follow.

On the SAT, you'll be expected to recognize the lack of parallelism. In some cases, you'll have to choose the best option for achieving the smoothest and most effective way of expressing an idea through parallel constructions.

LESSON 17: MISTAKES
WITH IDIOMS AND DICTION

Mistakes With Idioms

An idiom is "a form of expression, construction, phrase, etc., peculiar to a language" (*Shorter Oxford English Dictionary*).

As we begin our lesson on the correct phrasing of English idioms, we need to keep several things in mind. First, the most common mistakes involving English idioms occur when the idiom contains a preposition. Not surprisingly, the SAT will likely focus on these kinds of mistakes. Consider this example:

I was **angry at** my brother for his view on taxes.

While the expression may sound all right, the phrasing of the idiom is actually incorrect. The correct expression reads:

I was *angry with* my brother for his view on healthcare.

Correct usage requires us to hold to this distinction: we get *angry with* people, but we *get angry at* or *about* circumstances or actions.

Including the correct preposition in an English verb phrase is clearly not a matter of instinct or intuition, so we cannot rely on how the phrase sounds. The second point to keep in mind is that the multiple-choice portions of the SAT's writing section will probably contain several errors with English idioms—the ones that writers seem to have the most difficulty with and that you will be expected to recognize on the test. Finally, the following list of idioms that I've compiled for this lesson is NOT exhaustive; however, it does reflect the idioms that we use often in our writing and that I've often noticed in the practice tests of SAT prep books. The proper phrasing of the idioms is put in boldface and italicized.

A person may *accede to* someone else's wishes.

"Aggravate" and "irritate" do NOT mean the same thing even though people, mistakenly, use these verbs interchangeably. We use "aggravate" when an existing problem—an insect bite, an unfair situation at work, and so on—is made worse. The initial bite from a mosquito may *irritate* our skin, but, when we scratch that bite, we will probably *aggravate* it, that is, make it worse.

We *agree with* people, but we *agree to* a formal proposal, like a contract offer or proposed law. We *agree on* a course of action.

Fielding gets *angry with* his neighbor, but I get *angry about* the constant impasse in Congress: nothing ever seems to get done. Finally, I get *angry at* the constant talking in class that distracts serious students from their work.

There's no need to get *anxious about* taking the exam, but I am *eager to* go on vacation.
["Anxious" suggests "anxiety," tension, or perhaps even slight fear, while "eager" has a positive meaning and suggests anticipation, i.e., when we look forward to something positive happening, for example, "I am *eager to* go to homecoming." In summary, the words "anxious" and "eager" connote different feelings and should not be used interchangeably.]

I often *argue with* my best friend who is against supporting a local rescue shelter for abandoned animals.

The difference *between you AND me* is that you know how to prepare for the exam.

[Notice that the correct expression is *between you AND me.* The expression, "the difference between you OR me," IS WRONG.]

You and I are *capable of* improv*ing* our writing skills. [The proper idiom is "capable of" followed by a gerund—like "improving," or "skiing."]

The first day of our vacation *coincides with* the first day of the Lunar New Year.

A philosopher might *commune with* nature, and let's hope that she is *compatible with* her spouse.

Their best friends might *commiserate with* them over the loss of their beloved dog, but their neighbor might be *complacent about* any neighborhood clean-up efforts.

You might *compete with* your best friend in a friendly tennis match, but you would NEVER *compete against* your friend. We *comply with* requirements, and our lives should always *comport with* the highest ethical standards.

When do you use *compare to* and when do you use *compare with*? One of today's most respected authorities on American usage, Bryan Garner, says that the traditional school assignment "to compare and constrast is an English teacher's tautology" (that is, it doesn't make any sense) since to *compare with* actually means to put two things side by side and examine their similarities as well as their differences. So *compare with* does the job of both comparing (that is, showing similarities) and contrasting (that is, showing differences). The phrase *compare to* should be used for situations when writers want to emphasize only similarities or likenesses between two objects. The two examples that follow illustrate proper usage of these two phrases and are taken from *Garner's Modern American Usage*, Third Edition, Oxford: "let us *compare* his goals *with* his actual accomplishments" (similarities and differences) and "he *compared* her eyes *to* limpid pools" (similarities only).

I get **concerned about** the health of my best friend who never takes care of himself, but he and I continue to be **concerned with** the issue of humane treatment of animals. [Note that we are concerned about—meaning "worried about"—people and their *health, safety,* or *wellbeing,* but we are concerned with—meaning "involved with"—*issues, fields of study,* or *causes.*]

We **concur with** people on issues, but we **concur in** (i.e., agree on) a course of action or a proposal.

Some claim that a plant-based diet—one without meat, fish, or dairy products—is **conducive to** good health.

When you **confide in** your best friend, you're **confident of** his or her honoring your secret.

My sister will probably **consent to** her neighbor's request to let him use her backyard to store lumber, temporarily, for his remodeling project. Her decision is **consistent with** her belief that one should be a good neighbor. Not allowing her neighbor to store his lumber in her yard would be **inconsistent with** her belief.

A weak, insecure supervisor might become **contemptuous of** employees who get praise from the company's president.

One found guilty of armed robbery is **convicted of** a felony. Another may be **charged with** first-degree murder and is awaiting trial.

A sociopath is **devoid of** any remorse for even the most horrific crimes.

A Hybrid car *differs from* an all-electric vehicle in several features, but I *differ with* my brother about tax reform. [We never say "differ about."]

We would say that lyric poetry is *different from* epic poetry in a number of ways. ["Lyric poetry is 'different than' epic poetry in a number of ways" is wrong!]

She would never *dream of* hurting anyone's feelings.

The correct expressions are always, *either…or* or *neither…nor*, but never: "either…and" or "neither…and" or "either…nor" or "neither…or."

The prefix *e-* or *ex-* is taken from the Latin preposition meaning "from." Not surprisingly then, many of our English verbs that begin with the *e-* or *ex-* prefix are followed by the preposition "from." For instance, the player who shoved a referee was *ejected from* the game. Two boys were *expelled from* school for bullying other students. Cultural anthropologists *excavated* several artifacts *from* the site. I didn't think my brother would come and was surprised when I saw him finally *emerge from* the bus. Toxic gasses were being *emitted from* the smoke stacks. Also, my grandparents *emigrated from* Ireland, and they *immigrated to* the United States. [Don't use "out of" with any of these *e-* or *ex-* verbs. Use "from" instead.]

My brother *excels in* math and science while both my sisters *excel in* art.

I might complain that our team is *far from* living up to its potential. [I wouldn't say, "our team is far away from living up to its potential."]

The kitten was *fascinated with* the spider. She has a *fascination for* anything that moves.

Jack has a *fear of* heights. His sister has a *fear of* water.

My brother-in-law has a *fondness for* dogs. My sister is *fond of* cats.

Our nation was *founded on* principles that acknowledge and protect certain inalienable rights.

One of our rights is the *freedom of* expression, but one gains *freedom from* debilitating obsessions by means of therapy.

People may be *frightened by* lightning, but they are *afraid of* flash flooding. [The expression "frightened of" is wrong.]

We *graduate from* college. Careful writers use the verb phrase "graduate from" and avoid using the verb "graduate" as a transitive verb, as in "we graduated college." The *New Oxford American Dictionary* lists that latter usage as "informal," and usage authorities are not yet giving it a "thumbs up." Therefore, use the verb properly, as in "I *graduated from* college in 2012." Even though more and more people, including news anchors and journalists, are carelessly using the verb "graduate" as a transitive verb, you don't have to follow suit. You can be more careful. Use "graduate from," and avoid the "cutesy"shorthand "graduate college" in your writing, and be sure to recognize that usage as an error on the SAT .

Mary deeply loves her parents, but she is determined to become *independent of* them and make her own way financially in life. [Don't use "independent from."]

I am *grateful to* my parents for everything that they've done for me. I am *grateful for* the chances that I have had to pursue an education. [Remember that we are *grateful to* people and *grateful for* things.]

He *knows how to* conduct research. [The sentence, "he knows how conducting research" is obviously wrong.]

The basement is *impervious to* seepage because of the sealant we used to cover every crack and fissure. Some writers apply "impervious" to people's thinking, as in, he is "impervious to" reason. In other words, logic can't penetrate that hard head of his; however, "impervious to" should not be extended to feelings. Use *unaffected* instead. Therefore, a hardheaded friend is *impervious to* a reasonable argument that challenges his position, but a thick-skinned person is *unaffected by* criticism.

I hope that I'm not *imposing on* you. The instructor has tried to *impress on* us the importance of taking careful notes during lab work so that we can *improve on* last semester's performance.

When the senator lied about his *connection with* a wealthy financier, his dishonesty was *incongruous with* (inconsistent with) his campaign pledge that he would *adhere to* the highest standards of integrity.

They practiced piano several hours every day *in pursuit of* excellence.

We are *in search of* the truth. [Don't say or write "in search for" the truth.]

After several years of casework, the sociologist gained a clear *insight into* the difficulties of the poor.

Derrick often manages to *break free from* work to spend extra time with his children. [Note: It's wrong to write, "Derrick often manages breaking free from work."]

The senator used the idiom correctly when she said, "I *object to* that proposed amendment."

When I intend to do something, I *plan to do* it. When I *count on* or *rely on* something, that is, when I'm confident or fairly certain that something will happen, I *plan on* it happening, for instance, "I *plan on* your being there to help me. Don't let me down."

I *prefer* one thing *to* another. (I *prefer* soccer *to* baseball.)

Annual flu shots *protect* most people *from* the flu virus. The shots, however, do NOT "protect against" the virus.

People *protest against* injustices. People don't "protest over" injustices.

A relentlessly demanding swim coach might be *regarded as* a tyrant by some, but he would never be "regarded to be" a tyrant.

I *think it wise to do* something. [The idiom "think it wise" should be followed by an infinitive, "to do," "to develop," "to study," and so on, not a gerund—an "-ing" form of the verb.]

A dangerous object, a virus, or a bacterium can be a *threat to* someone, not a "threat of" someone.

We use things or processes *to accomplish* something. [We never use things or processes "in the accomplishing" of something.]

How do you use the preceding list as you prepare for the SAT? I suggest that you read through this list of correct idioms, which are both italicized and put in boldface, several times as soon as possible. In that way, you will have the proper phrasing of idioms "echoing" in your short-term memory. To retain them in your long-term memory, read them again occasionally. In that way, with repetition, you'll be more likely to recognize a misused idiom on the SAT and be able to correct or avoid misused idioms in your own writing.

Mistakes with Diction

Certain words in English, because they sound alike or look alike, often get confused. You can expect that one or several of these words will be included on the SAT to test your knowledge of correct usage. These errors in diction are included in practically every handbook or grammar book on the market. Look at my "Books I Recommend" section for several good ones. The following list of easily confused words is not exhaustive, but it does reflect the errors in diction that I've often seen in students' essays, that I myself have been guilty of and edited out of my own work, and that seem to mar the work of writers in high school and college:

Accept; except.
To "accept" something is to consent to receive it, as in this sentence, "I *accept* your offer of employment," or when you own up to something, for example, "I *accept* responsibility for those uncorrected errors in the newsletter." "Accept" can also mean "to tolerate or submit to something unpleasant or undesired," as in the sentence, "I *accept* defeat." "Except" refers to an "exception," when something is left out, not involved, or excluded, for instance, "everyone went to the game *except* Roger who stayed at home."

Abjure; adjure.
I'll be honest with you. I have to look up these words every time I come across them. To "abjure" is to formally or solemnly renounce a belief, for instance, "Sir Thomas More refused to *abjure* his Roman Catholic faith." To "adjure" is to urge or request under very formal circumstances (a proceeding, a hearing, an investigation) to do something. "I *adjure* you to give us the facts."

Adverse; averse.
The adjective, "adverse" means "harmful, unfavorable, or hostile." "Rising gasoline prices are having an *adverse* effect on the economy." The adjective "averse" means "opposed." "I am not *averse* to spending money on books, but I am *averse* to wasting money on DVDs. I never watch them more than once after I buy them."

Affect; effect.
As a noun, "affect" refers to an emotion, visible to others, for instance, "the patient was expressionless: she showed no *affect* at

all." As a noun, "effect" refers to a "result" of something else, for instance, "the *effects* (i.e., results) of her unorthodox diet were severe headaches and insomnia." As verbs, "affect" and "effect" differ as follows: When I am *affected* by something, I am influenced by it, or I am emotionally stirred by it, for example, "Her rudeness *affected* (i.e., influenced) my decision not to buy any of her products," and "the film *affected* (i.e., moved) me deeply." To "effect" something is to cause it to happen, for instance, "the aerospace industry has *effected* (i.e., caused) many changes in the computer industry."

Alumnus; alumni; alumna; alumnae
I'm certain that you've heard someone say proudly, "I'm an alumni of...." For the sake of the example, let's say it's Yale University. You might be impressed with the person's *alma mater*, but you know immediately that she or he never studied Latin at New Haven. An "alumnus" is ONE male graduate of a school. The word is the masculine singular form of the Latin word meaning "a nursling, a pupil." "Alumni," on the other hand, are graduates, and the word is the plural form of the Latin word. It's ironic that those with college degrees often don't make the distinction correctly. Never say or write, "I am an alumni of..." You are an *alumnus* (if a man) or an *alumna* (if a woman). Use *alumnae* for women graduates. Use *alumni* for men graduates and for men and women graduates collectively.

Complement; compliment.
To "compliment" someone is to give that person praise as in, "I *complimented* him on an outstanding performance." "He graciously received many *compliments* for his work on the stage." To "complement" is "to add something in a way that enhances or improves it, to make perfect" (*New Oxford American Dictionary*). "The hard-nosed running of Alfred Morris *complements* Robert Griffin III's precise passing to give the team an effective offense."

Criterion; phenomenon; datum.
Each one of these words—*criterion, phenomenon, datum*—is singular. (The plural forms of these words are "criteria, data, and

phenomena" respectively.) If you're speaking of only one standard of behavior or evaluation, you would use "criterion," for instance, "the last *criterion* for our evaluation is the applicant's fluency in Mandarin." You and I probably wouldn't want to work for a company that misused "criterion," and wrote, "the last criteria for our evaluation is the applicant's fluency in Mandarin." Similarly, we should say or write, "the *phenomenon* of a solar eclipse is rare." It is INCORRECT to say or write, "the phenomena of a solar eclipse is rare," yet we hear that mistake made far too often on commercial television. When scientists speak of one piece of information, they refer to it as a "datum." "Data," on the other hand, is plural, and, if you see "data" as a subject of a clause on the SAT, make sure that its verb or its pronoun agrees with it in number, for instance, "all the *data have been collected* for the experiment, and *they* are ready to be analyzed."

Fewer; less.
"Less" can be an adjective and modify noncount nouns, for instance, "there is *less* gasoline in the car than I thought." "Less" can also be used as an adverb, as in "they worked far *less* than before." "Fewer" is used with count nouns: "no *fewer* than twenty applicants have submitted proposals to do work with our company," and "*fewer* people subscribe to newspapers than ever before." So when you see a sign over the checkout line at your grocery store, "EXPRESS LANE, ten or **less** items," you know that it's grammatically incorrect, and you'll no doubt avoid making a similar mistake in your own writing.

Absolutes: words that do not take comparatives or superlatives

There are a number of words that shouldn't be written as comparatives or superlatives.

If something is *unique*, for example, it is one of a kind. Hence, to say "more unique," "most unique," "least unique," or "less unique," defies logic, so avoid the comparative or superlative forms of *unique*. If something's *unique*, that's it. That same absolute quality (not allowing a comparison) also applies to "full."

I'm certain that you've heard or read something like this sentence, "she covered the topic more fully than the other author." If someone did something completely or fully how can he or she add anything to it? Doesn't the writer really mean, "she covered the topic *more extensively*" or "she covered the topic in *greater detail* than the other author"? If so, then the writer should be precise and say it in one of those two ways. Don't follow the crowd. Be precise in your word selection. [I'll let you in on a secret: I almost wrote, without thinking just then, "more precise." That would have run counter to my own advice. If something is *precise* or *exact*, then it's on target. It's perfect, and perfection can't be improved: it can't be "more" or "most" precise.]

Another word that can't have a comparative form is *fatal*. The word "fatal" relates to death, as in "the wound was fatal." One injury or action therefore can't be more fatal than another. In other words, it can't cause more death to an individual. Dead is dead, and fatal is fatal, so don't try to make a comparative out of that word. The wound was *fatal*, and that's it. Never say or write, "more fatal" or "most fatal."

Someone might be ecstatic after a date with her new boyfriend and say euphorically, "it was the most perfect day I've ever had in my life." Not to suck all the air out of festivities or anything, but I have to interject a little realism here. Like the words "fatal" and "unique," "perfect" is *perfect* and can't by definition be or get any better. The young woman would be correct just saying, "the day was *perfect*." Let perfection speak for itself.

Equal is another word that can't logically have a comparative form. Yes, I know that in George Orwell's *Animal Farm*, Napoleon and his corrupt followers come up with the slogan, "All animals are equal, but some are more equal than others." Orwell creates the absurd, illogical phrase "more equal" to show the reader just how ridiculous, corrupt, and dishonest the leaders of the animal farm have become. [Theodore M. Bernstein cites this example from *Animal Farm* in his entry on "equal" in *The Careful Writer*.] So, if your grades are *equal* to your brother's, neither his grades nor your grades are higher or lower than the other's. They're the *same*; his grades can never be more equal than your grades or vice versa.

Formally; formerly.
The adverb, "formerly" refers to earlier times, as in the sentence, "she was *formerly* a State senator. Now she is a Member of the House of Representatives." The adverb "formally" refers to "in accordance with the rules of convention or etiquette," as in the sentence, "he was *formally* attired." The word, "formally" can also mean "officially," as in the sentence, "the mayor will *formally* open the new railroad station." (The material on these two "sound-alike" adverbs is taken verbatim from the *New Oxford American Dictionary*.)

Imply; infer.
These two verbs are frequently confused. A speaker or a writer *implies* or *suggests* something. An audience or a reader *infers* or *draws a conclusion* from something that a speaker or writer has suggested. So if you read, "the writer inferred that we should be more prudent in how we preserve the environment," get out the red pen and change "inferred" to "implied." In short, speakers and writers *imply* (suggest). Listeners and readers *infer* (draw conclusions).

Respectively; respectfully.
The adverb "respectively" means separately and individually AND in the order already mentioned. The meaning of the sentence, "Johnson and Adams received sentences of fifteen years and five years *respectively*" is that Johnson got a fifteen-year sentence and Adams, the second convicted criminal who was mentioned, got a five-year sentence.

Respectfully, on the other hand, means, showing respect toward something or someone else, as in this sentence:

> They *respectfully* stood in silence in front of the Vietnam War Memorial.

To become a better writer, become a better reader.

LESSON 18: RELATIVES...
WHICH... THAT... WHO

In English, we use the term "relative pronoun" to refer to a word that: 1. relates to a previous word in the sentence, and 2. takes the place of a noun or a pronoun. In the following sentence, the relative pronoun is "who" and its antecedent is "exciting quarterback":

antecedent   *relative pronoun*
↓   ↓

RGIII is *an exciting quarterback, who* was the second overall pick in the NFL's 2012 draft.

Here are some follow-up points to keep in mind:

Use the relative pronoun "who" or "whom" to refer to a person or to people.

Use the relative pronoun "which" to refer to a thing or things.

Use the relative pronoun "that" to refer to a thing or to things, or when a group is involved. ("The *team that* wins the most games in its division goes to the playoffs.) [The source of this explanation is the *St. Martin's Handbook, 5th Edition*]

So if you come across sentences like these on the SAT, know that the incorrect relative pronouns are being used and need to be corrected:

A. Don Williams, **that** wrote the best short story, will earn $100 in prize money. (Wrong)

B. Teddy Roosevelt and John Fitzgerald Kennedy are presidents, **which** I admire. (No)

Here are the correct versions of the preceding sentences:

A. Don Williams, *who* wrote the best short story, will earn $100 in prize money. (Yes)

B. Teddy Roosevelt and John Fitzgerald Kennedy are presidents *whom* I admire. (Yes)

There are also in English relative adverbs—words that relate, for our purposes, to places and times. Use the relative adverb "when" to refer to a point in or period of time and "where" to refer to a place or location. The following sentence is wrong and needs to be corrected:

The 18th century, **where** many current grammatical rules were set down, is referred to as the Age of Reason. (Wrong)

Here's the obvious correction:

The 18th century, *when* many current grammatical rules were set down, is referred to as the Age of Reason. (Correct)

Use the relative adverb "where" to refer to a place or places. Look at this little gem:

When did he meet his wife? **In** Germany.

Being in Germany may have defined a particular time in the man's life, but Germany is not a time; it's a place. The correct version of the sentence above is:

> *Where* did he meet his wife? *In* Germany.

There's one final point to remember about "where" and "when." Never use "where" or "when" to define a term. Never say,

> Apnea is **when** you have long pauses in your breathing during sleep,

or

> Apnea is **where** you have long pauses in your breathing during sleep.

Little kids define things that way. Such attempts at definitions sound very young and have no place in high school or college writing. To define a term properly, use a *genus* (class) and a *species* (the particular details that separate the item from the other members of the class). An appropriate way to define the above example is as follows:

> Apnea is a temporary cessation of breathing[1] especially during sleep[2] (*New Oxford American Dictionary*).

---

[1] genus: *cessation of breathing*

[2] species: *temporary, during sleep*

If you give Relax I *a chance, you'll be pleased with the results.*

SELF-ASSESSMENT

Here's the self-assessment that I mentioned in Lesson 14. I recommend that you use this assessment as a guide to understand how well you've mastered the lessons on grammar and style that we've covered in *Relax I* and what review and follow-up work you may need to do. I have included a list of the errors that we discussed in *Relax I*. Referring to that list, identify any error in grammar or style that is present in each of the following sentences. There will be a space for your correction of any error that you find. There are several sentences that are correct and free of any errors in style or grammar. For error-free sentences, simply put a "C" in the first blank.

EXAMPLE: Mark driving to California.

Sentence Fragment   is driving____
ERROR   **CORRECTION**

EXAMPLE: Across the river grow many unusual plants.

___C___   _____
ERROR   **CORRECTION**

ERRORS WE'VE COVERED:

1. Misplaced Modifiers

2. Wordiness

3. Errors with Verb Tenses

4. Sentence Fragments

5. Comma Splices and Run-On Sentences

6. Errors with Double Negatives

7. The "Between-You-and-I" Error

8. Unclear Pronoun References

9. Inconsistent Pronouns

10. Faulty Comparisons

11. The "2-is-not-1" Error

12. Mistakes with Adverbs and Adjectives

13. "Who" vs. "Whom"

14. Lack of Agreement of a Verb with its Subject

15. Lack of Agreement of a Pronoun with its Antecedent

16. Lack of Parallelism

17. Mistakes with Idioms and Diction

18. Relatives... Which... That... Who

1. The president of our homeowners association inferred that most of us were unwilling to volunteer time for the benefit of the community.

———————————————   ———————————————

ERROR   **CORRECTION**

2. Beyond the mountains lie rich pastureland.

———————————————   ———————————————

ERROR   **CORRECTION**

3. The university has announced that they are going to increase tuition for a third time in four years.

———————————————   ———————————————

ERROR   **CORRECTION**

4. I finished the exam before the proctor called for the tests.

———————————————   ———————————————

ERROR   **CORRECTION**

5. The competition is down to just two contestants. Either you or John are the winner.

———————————————   ———————————————

ERROR   **CORRECTION**

6. Neither Brad's parents nor Brad takes the time to walk the family dog.

———————————————   ———————————————

ERROR   **CORRECTION**

7. Al Gore, as well as John McCain, feel that Presidential elections should be determined, not by electoral votes, but by the total number of votes cast nationwide.

_____   _____

ERROR   **CORRECTION**

8. The tennis pro missed shot after shot; he was uncharacteristic inaccurate in today's match.

_____   _____

ERROR   **CORRECTION**

9. Senator Barbara Mikulski and Senator Ben Cardin have served in the U.S. Senate for twenty-six and seven years respectfully.

_____   _____

ERROR   **CORRECTION**

10. I implied from the speaker's remarks that he really didn't have a high regard for the works of Jeremy Taylor.

_____   _____

ERROR   **CORRECTION**

11. The works of the British poets of the 20th-century, which wrote traditional verse as well as free verse, are included in our literature book.

_____   _____

ERROR   **CORRECTION**

12. The Leonardtown Raiders are Sandy's favorite team while my favorite team is the Raritan Tigers.

_____   _____
ERROR   **CORRECTION**

13. Neither Brad's parents nor Brad drives to work. All three take public transportation.

_____   _____
ERROR   **CORRECTION**

14. The principal qualities of his fiction are well-constructed plots, exotic settings, and how realistic all of his characters seem to be.

_____   _____
ERROR   **CORRECTION**

15. The investigator who leads a team of four junior police officers are dedicated to apprehending those responsible for a string of burglaries in Chevy Chase, Maryland.

_____   _____
ERROR   **CORRECTION**

16. Neither Brad nor his parents drives to work. All three take public transportation.

_____   _____
ERROR   **CORRECTION**

17. O'Hara and Bernstein* is selling all of their winter clothing at considerable discounts. (*O'Hara and Bernstein is a store.)

_____   _____
ERROR   **CORRECTION**

18. Gerard Manley Hopkins and John Donne are known for their startling figures of speech and the deeply religious themes of their poems.

_____   _____
ERROR   **CORRECTION**

19. In spite of her frequent objections that the trip was too expensive, Artemis decided at the last minute to go with Sarah and I to the Grand Canyon.

_____   _____
ERROR   **CORRECTION**

20. After the investigation, the police determined that the culprit was neither Jack or his roommate.

_____   _____
ERROR   **CORRECTION**

21. After marking all of the students' tests, it became very clear to me that no one had taken the assessment all that seriously.

_____   _____
ERROR   **CORRECTION**

22. We were pleased with the way Dr. Patel treated us as patients we recommended him to our neighbors.

_____   _____
ERROR   **CORRECTION**

23. The affects of poor diet and no exercise are often diabetes and high blood pressure.

    _____   _____

    ERROR   **CORRECTION**

24. In the event that you should be presented with an offer of employment, you would do well to accept it.

    _____   _____

    ERROR   **CORRECTION**

25. One should never carry on a conversation during a lecture. You could run the risk of being asked to leave the auditorium.

    _____   _____

    ERROR   **CORRECTION**

26. Mrs. Campbell called Mrs. Ratcliff to complain that her son is not studying as hard as he should.

    _____   _____

    ERROR   **CORRECTION**

27. Because I have studied all night. I am exhausted.

    _____   _____

    ERROR   **CORRECTION**

28. Fourteen small companies submitted their bid to manage the dormitories for the university.

    _____   _____

    ERROR   **CORRECTION**

29. There are at least four people whom I think should be honored this year by the commissioners for their work to help abused women in our county.

_____   _____

ERROR   **CORRECTION**

30. One should follow all of the company's policies and directives; otherwise, you might receive a poor rating from your supervisor.

_____   _____

ERROR   **CORRECTION**

31. The spoiled meat smelled badly, but the fish tasted delicious.

_____   _____

ERROR   **CORRECTION**

32. I hardly didn't sleep at all last night.

_____   _____

ERROR   **CORRECTION**

33. Our new director, Andrea Salter, which graduated from Dunbarton College, went to school with my uncle.

_____   _____

ERROR   **CORRECTION**

34. Everyone who saw the film were affected by the final scene.

_____   _____

ERROR   **CORRECTION**

35. The pitching rotation of the Leonardtown Raiders is not quite as impressive this year as the Lexington Park Cardinals.

_____   _____
ERROR   **CORRECTION**

36. The number of students who are taking AP English classes has decreased since 2010.

_____   _____
ERROR   **CORRECTION**

37. Using our binoculars, the mountains seemed to be just a few hundred yards away from us.

_____   _____
ERROR   **CORRECTION**

38. My supervisor is impressed with John, a new applicant for the job, because John is an alumni of American University.

_____   _____
ERROR   **CORRECTION**

39. Charles Dickens, who helped effect social change during England's Industrial Revolution by means of his novels, were praised by audiences throughout Europe and North America.

_____   _____
ERROR   **CORRECTION**

40. A number of students has submitted applications for off-campus housing for the fall semester.

_____   _____
ERROR   **CORRECTION**

ANSWERS TO THE SELF-ASSESSMENT

1. Mistake with Idioms and Diction; "implied" (not "inferred") is the correct word.

2. Lack of Agreement of a Verb with its Subject; "lies" (not "lie")

3. Lack of Agreement of a Pronoun with its Antecedent; "it is going" (not "they are going")

4. Wrong Verb Tense; "I had finished" (not "I finished")

5. Lack of Agreement of a Verb with its Subject: "John is" (not "John are")

6. Correct

7. Lack of Agreement of a Verb with its Subject; "Al Gore... feels" (not "feel")

8. Confusion of Adjective and Adverb; "uncharacteristically inaccurate" (not "uncharacteristic inaccurate")

9. Mistake with Idioms and Diction; "respectively" (not "respectfully")

10. Mistake with Idioms and Diction; "inferred" (not "implied")

11. Wrong Relative pronoun; "who wrote" (not "which wrote")

12. Correct

13. Correct

14. Lack of Parallelism; "realism of his characters" (not "how realistic his characters are")

15. Lack of Agreement of a Verb with its Subject; "is dedicated" (not "are dedicated")

16. Lack of Agreement of a Verb with its Subject; "parents drive" (not "parents drives")

17. Lack of Agreement of a Pronoun with its Antecedent: "its winter clothing" (not "their winter clothing")

18. Correct

19. The "Between-You-and-I Error;" "go with Sarah and me" (not "with Sarah and I")

20. Lack of Parallelism; "neither Jack nor his roommate" (not "or his roommate")

21. Misplaced Modifier; "I realized" (not "it became clear to me")

22. Run-on sentence; put a period after "patients" and begin a new sentence with "We recommended."

23. A Mistake with Idioms and Diction; "effects of poor diet…" (not "affects")

24. Wordiness. Change "In the event that" to "if."

25. Inconsistent Pronoun; make the references either "one…one" or "you…you."

26. Unclear Pronoun Reference. Change "her son" to either "Mrs. Campbell's son" or "Mrs. Ratcliff's son."

27. Sentence Fragment. Combine the dependent clause with the independent clause to form one sentence: "Because I studied all night, I am exhausted."

28. The "2-is-not-1" Error; "fourteen…companies submitted their bids" (not "bid")

29. When to Use "Who" and When to Use "Whom;" "who I think" (not "whom I think")

30. Inconsistent Pronoun; "You should follow" (not "one should follow")

31. Confusion of Adverb and Adjective; "smelled bad" (not "smelled badly")

32. Error with a Double Negative; "I hardly slept" (not "I hardly didn't sleep")

33. Wrong Relative Pronoun; "who graduated" (not "which graduated")

34. Lack of Agreement of a Verb with its Subject; "Everyone…was affected" (not "everyone…were affected")

35. Faulty Comparison; "as that of the Lexington Park Cardinals" (not simply "the Lexington Park Cardinals"). Compare a pitching rotation with a pitching rotation, not with a team.

36. Correct

37. Misplaced Modifier; "Using our binoculars, we noticed" (not "Using our binoculars, the mountains….")

38. A Mistake with Idioms and Diction: the man is an "alumnus" (not "alumni")

39. Lack of Agreement of a Verb with its Subject; "Charles Dickens...was praised" (not "were praised")

40. Lack of Agreement of a Verb with Its Subject; "A number of students" is plural. Therefore, the verb should be "have submitted" (not "has submitted.")

NOTE: For any of the answers that you missed, go back to the appropriate lesson and review the material so that you'll understand the reason for the correct answer.

PART II: ESSAY WRITING

Reading and Writing

If you want to become a better writer, you have to become a better reader. In other words, you have to read more and read actively, **every day**, to improve your writing. You've undoubtedly heard the expression, "you are what you eat," which applies to your physical health. I would add, for the health of your mind and your spirit, you are what you read. If a person reads only sloppy, silly, immature, or even base material, she or he will produce, not surprisingly, sloppy, silly, immature, or base writing. You're better than that, so keep in mind what the poet Jane Kenyon advises, "Have good sentences in your ears."[1] Where do you find "good" sentences? You find them in the works of skilled authors whose writings should be used as models, not only by beginning writers but by anyone who aspires to become an accomplished writer.

You may have noticed that in the previous paragraph I underlined "every day" and put it in boldface. I want to stress that it's not only what you read but how often you read that will shape you as a writer. Reading assigned novels once or twice a quarter won't get the job done. You know that if you exercise only when you feel like it, you won't get in shape, and sporadic workouts certainly won't help you become a decent athlete. As it is with exercise and health, so it is with reading and writing.

---

[1] Quoted by Samuel Cohen in *50 Essays: A Portable Anthology*

To develop your writing skills, you have to make a commitment to read writing of high quality every day. The term "writing of high quality" is subject to different opinions. If English teachers were asked to compile a list of works of fiction and non-fiction that high school students should read as part of their preparation for college, there would of course be disagreement; however, there would also be a surprising number of books, essays, and speeches that would appear on every list. At the end of this section, I've included a selective (far from exhaustive) list of works that I feel a high school student should read in preparation for college.

Daily Reading and Writing

The daily reading that I urge you to do must go hand-in-hand with daily writing. Writing is a skill. To develop that skill, you must practice it every day. Do what the great ones have done before you. Keep a journal and include everything that you write: your creative work, your positions on essential issues, national events, or even the events at your school or in your neighborhood. Write opinion pieces and add them to your journal. Write about things that interest you, the things that anger you, the things that you love. If you post your opinions on blogs, write as if you were addressing not your peers but the admissions officer of the college or university that you want to attend. (That doesn't mean that you have to use big words. It simply means to be careful when you write and follow the guidelines that we've gone over together.)

Your development as a writer won't happen overnight. Becoming a better writer will take time and require effort, but patient perseverance will pay off. In time, you'll be pleased with the improvement in your writing—both in the ease with which you write and in the quality of your writing. You'll have much more to say and be able to say it much better. You'll also notice, in time, that what you write will be clearer and more unified, more cohesive and more interesting— both in the way you build your sentences and in the turn you give your phrases. You'll find that choosing the precise word to convey exactly what you want to say will come easier. You'll start to develop your own voice and your own style. Conversely, trying to write without reading great literature—both ancient and modern—is like trying to carry on a conversation with an uninformed person: the conversation will be dull and uninspiring. So read and write every day. That commitment will pay off for you now, in college, in life, and, more to the point, on the SAT.

Connection with the SAT

While the long-term goal of our work is to improve your writing for college and beyond, we do have a short-term goal in front of us: SAT preparation. In Part I, we focused on the multiple-choice writing portions of the SAT, which focus on English grammar and preferred style. Now, we'll look at how to prepare for the essay assignment on the SAT— both in the coming days and during the exam itself.

Documenting What You Read

In the coming days, I would like you to start keeping a record of what you read in school and on your own. I encourage you to make note cards (3x5 or 4x6 inch cards will do nicely) to document several things about the works you read: the title, the author, its genre (whether it's an essay, a novel, a speech, etc.), a brief summary of the work, its major theme(s), and any of your observations about the work. I suggest that you also add any quotation from the work that impresses you and that seems to capture the central theme of the work. (An electronic file will work well too.) It sounds like a lot of work. Actually, it will take about fifteen minutes to document a work.

The following page shows an example of a note card for "Shooting an Elephant" by George Orwell. I recommend that you document your reading in a similar way.

> "Shooting an Elephant" (an essay), George Orwell
>
> SUMMARY: The narrator was a colonial police officer in Burma. He killed an elephant, not because the animal was dangerous, but because the Burmese wanted and expected him to kill it.
>
> THEME: Under pressure from others, people can do disturbing things that are against their beliefs.
>
> QUOTATION: "And suddenly I realized that I should have to shoot the elephant after all. The people expected it of me and I had got to do it; I could feel their two thousand wills pressing me forward, irresistibly."
>
> PERSONAL OBSERVATION: What's disturbing about the narrator's lack of courage is that he killed the elephant because people expected it AND because he didn't want to look like a fool. WOW! That's chilling.

After a while, you will begin to see and document common themes that are treated in literature. For example, if you were to read and then add notes on "Salvation," by Langston Hughes and on Mark Twain's *Adventures of Huckleberry Finn*, you would recognize similar themes dealing with the expectations of others, including the demands of the law, versus one's conscience. The notes on these two works might look like the examples on the following pages.

"Salvation" (an essay), Langston Hughes

SUMMARY: The narrator is a 13-year old boy who is taken to church and is expected to show everyone present that he has been saved by walking up to the altar with others his age. He doesn't feel saved, yet he's aware of the pressure with everyone in the church waiting for him to act so he does what he doesn't believe. He does what is expected of him. He feels like a cheat, starts to cry, and blames God for his lack of faith. Ironically, others think his tears stem from his conversion.

side 1

"Salvation" (an essay), Langston Hughes

THEME: Under pressure from others, people can do things that are expected of them rather than what they truly believe.

QUOTATION: "I began to be ashamed of myself, holding everything up so long…so I got up."

PERSONAL OBSERVATION: [This essay is like "Shooting an Elephant"—pressure from others can drive a person to do what's wrong or, in this case, what he doesn't believe.]

side 2

Adventures of Huckleberry Finn, Mark Twain

SUMMARY: The narrator, Huck Finn, is a runaway, first from two women who want to civilize him and then from his abusive father. Huck meets another runaway—Jim, a slave "owned" by one of the women who had custody of Huck. Huck and Jim flee down the Mississippi + have a number of adventures. In the end, Jim is freed, and Huck decides to flee to the Indian territory away from civilization.

THEMES:
1. Even under great pressure, truly good people follow their consciences rather than unfair laws or the expectations of others.
2. Slavery is evil and can never be defended.
3. Those who defend slavery in the novel are church-going hypocrites and blind to what they are doing. (The Grangerfords, the Widow Douglas, Miss Watson)

side 1

Adventures of Huckleberry Finn, Mark Twain

KEY EVENT: Huck lies and refuses to turn Jim, a runaway slave, over to the bounty hunters who want to return Jim to his "owner." Huck's refusal is against the law, but he does what he knows in his heart is right even though others say it's wrong and even though he wrongly thinks he will go to hell for disobeying the law.

PERSONAL OBSERVATION: The theme in the novel revolves around the conflict between what the law or society requires and what the individual knows to be right. This theme is also found in Dr. King's *Letter from Birmingham Jail* and Thoreau's *Civil Disobedience*.

side 2

I suggest that you record on note cards or store on your computer summaries of what you read for several reasons. Besides the long-term advantage of documenting your encounter with outstanding works, there is a practical, short-term advantage. The assigned essay on the SAT will ask you to take a position on a prompt—usually on a very broad topic. Because the topic is sufficiently broad, it gives you flexibility on how to approach the assignment. First of all, you must take a stand on the issue presented in the prompt. Then once you decide on a thesis and a clear position on the issue, you must support your position with examples from literature, history, current events, personal experience, or personal observation. By documenting what you read, you'll start to see and record frequently treated themes and various ways of looking at broad topics by great writers. That record is valuable in itself; however, for the near future, it will become a storehouse from which you can draw examples to support your position on the SAT's assigned essay prompt.

The Day of the Test: Let's Build Part of an SAT Essay

Your first assignment on the SAT will be to write an essay on an assigned topic. It's important to note that the topic is assigned to you. You have to respond to the prompt. You may not ignore it and write on a different topic. If you do, it will be the same as if you didn't write the essay at all: you will receive a zero. (I had a student whose SAT "essay" began with a rant against the prompt, namely, that the prompt was not a very good one, and that it could have been stated much better. He then covered what he wanted to write about. As you might have guessed, he received a zero. He lost 240 points from the outset of the test.) So it's important to play the game by the SAT's rules and write in response to the essay prompt.

With SAT essay prompts, there will be at least two "sides" to the issue. That flexibility allows you to choose a position. Your stance on the issue is of no concern to the essay graders. How you develop your answer is.

Let's take this hypothetical essay prompt to work with:

BACKGROUND

A government can operate effectively only when its citizens are law-abiding. For the common good, therefore, citizens need to comply with all the laws of a government.

ASSIGNMENT

Do citizens in fact need to comply with all the laws of a government? Plan and write an essay in which you develop your point of view on this issue. Support your position with reasoning and examples taken from literature, your studies, history, current events, personal experience, or observations.

These are the steps[1] that I recommend that you follow as you plan and write the essay for the SAT:

1. Focus on the prompt for a minute or two. Really concentrate on it. Don't skip over it or rush your focus. That focus will generate ideas. Your feelings about the topic will emerge and examples that support your position may also come to mind.

2. Then begin your planning. This step should also take only several minutes—two or three at the most. Write out your thesis, which reflects your position on the topic, and outline your essay. Just listing the examples that will support your position will do the job at this point.

3. Then devote the bulk of your time—about twenty minutes—to writing the essay. (The more you practice, on your own, in the

---

[1] I am suggesting that you use a four-step process to plan and write your SAT essay. That four-step process is adapted almost entirely from the suggestions for planning and writing the SAT essay found in Kaplan's *SAT 2010 Edition: Strategies, Practice, and Review*. I have also adhered to Kaplan's suggested time values to be followed for each step. Kaplan calls those steps the 4P's—"Prompt, Plan, Produce, and Proof." While I do not use those terms or abbreviations, my steps are derived from Kaplan's helpful SAT preparation book.

coming months, the easier it will be to plan and write an essay within the strict time limit of twenty-five minutes.)

4. When there's only a minute or two left, proofread your work for any glaring errors. Know that you won't lose points for a minor error, such as one misspelling or a minor grammatical lapse. On the other hand, if your essay is filled with misspellings and grammatical errors, it stands to reason your essay will receive a lower grade.

Approaching the Introduction

In the introduction of your essay, you MUST make your position on the issue clear. You have to take a stand. We all know that things are not always black or white. To be accurate sometimes, we have to acknowledge and grapple with "gray" areas, exceptions, and isolated examples. For the purposes of the SAT essay—I can't say this strongly enough—take a clear stand on the SAT essay assignment. Then stay with your position throughout the essay, and build a case to convince your reader that it makes sense for you to hold this position. Don't be "wishy-washy." Don't vacillate. Be firm. Take a position and maintain it. That's creating unity—one of the qualities that the essay graders are looking for. There are also practical reasons for choosing and developing one side of the issue presented in the SAT essay prompt. Twenty-five minutes to write an essay doesn't give you enough time to explore all the complexities of an issue. Dealing with "gray" areas requires that you qualify things, make exceptions, and make many distinctions—activities that take time, which, frankly, you don't have on the SAT.

Let's look at our hypothetical prompt again and start to build an essay together:

BACKGROUND

A government can operate effectively only when its citizens are law-abiding. For the common good, therefore, citizens need to comply with all the laws of a government.

125

ASSIGNMENT

Do citizens in fact need to comply with all the laws of a government? Plan and write an essay in which you develop your point of view on this issue. Support your position with reasoning and examples taken from literature, your studies, history, current events, personal experience, or observations.

Since there are several sides to this prompt, we would first have to decide whether we agree with the proposition that citizens have to obey all laws at all times or whether we believe citizens have the right to disobey laws, perhaps under unique circumstances. For the sake of argument, let's assume that we disagree with the statement in the prompt, and during our two-to-three-minute essay planning, we write out the following thesis statement: if a law is unfair or discriminates against people, citizens have not only the right, but also the duty to resist the law.

The stance that we've just taken is firm and leaves no room for doubt or misunderstanding about our position. It's a good start. Our thesis, however, was made in the context of a bigger idea, namely, that governments can only operate effectively when people obey laws. That bigger context shouldn't be ignored. Some writers have found that building into their opening a concession is an effective way to address this point. So, just before our thesis statement in the opening paragraph of our essay, let's add a concession statement, which says, in effect, you've got a point, but what I'm going to present is a better way to look at the issue. So your opening might look like this:

concession
↓

There would be chaos, of course, if citizens didn't obey the laws of their government,

but if a law is unfair, people have the right, even the duty,
to resist it.

↑

thesis

So far, the opening of our essay is taking shape: our position or
stance is clear, we're responding to the prompt, and we're offering
a concession so that our position is made within the general
background of that prompt. Also, we gain points from our
audience because when we acknowledge that the other side has a
valid point, we're communicating that we're fair, that we at least
listen to what the other side has to say, and that there may be
some merit in some of their views. If, as writers, we're fair and
open-minded, our readers will be more inclined to attend to what
we have to say. Who doesn't respect a fair, open-minded person?

Now we have to offer support for our thesis. Let's say that the
following two works come immediately to mind during our
planning, as we think about the prompt: Dr. Martin Luther King,
Jr.'s *Letter from Birmingham Jail* and Mark Twain's *Adventures of
Huckleberry Finn.*

These two works would definitely support the idea that resisting
an unfair law is sometimes necessary. One example from
American history might also come to mind during our planning:
the American colonists' resistance to the Stamp Act that Britain
unfairly imposed on the colonies. We might then add after our
thesis this statement which sets the stage for the examples that
we'll include in our essay's body: "At least two works of
American literature, and an event from America's own history,
offer convincing arguments that people have the right to resist
unjust laws for a greater purpose."

Our introduction would then read:

> There would be chaos, of course, if citizens didn't obey the
> laws of their government, but if a law is unfair, people
> have the right, even the duty, to resist it. At least two

works of American literature, and an event from America's own history, offer convincing arguments that people need to resist unjust laws for a greater purpose.

I think our essay is starting to look good. By adding that last sentence, we have provided an introduction for the examples in the essay's body that will build our case for the thesis.

Then using the outline that we made during our planning, we'll take each one of the works of literature and an event from American history to write the essay's body. Each example will form the topic that we'll develop to build our case and "prove" our point. The outline of our essay's body might look something like this:

First paragraph of the body: Huck Finn disobeys an unfair slave law to protect his friend.

Second paragraph of the body: Dr. King resists an unfair local law to support underpaid workers.

Third paragraph of the body: Americans revolt against England's unjust Stamp Act to defend their rights.

We will then add a conclusion that's the logical result of what we've said in our essay or that's a good summary of our position. Our conclusion might read something like:

> In summary, no one would suggest that citizens should disregard their nation's laws. When laws, however, discriminate against a certain group or race of people or when laws deprive people of their basic rights, citizens must defy those laws to achieve a greater good, for an unjust law is really no law at all.

[The statement "an unjust law is no law at all" is from St. Augustine, quoted by Dr. Martin Luther King, Jr. in *Letter from Birmingham Jail*.]

We've walked through the process of writing an SAT essay together. You know how to do it. The main issue on the day of the test will be the constraint of writing an essay in just twenty-five minutes. You'll reduce the pressure on yourself by practicing now. Try writing an essay within that time limit at least once a week. Type in the phrase "SAT essay prompts" in a web browser. You'll find many good sites with prompts for your practice essays.

The Week Prior to the Exam

If you follow my suggestions about documenting your readings in high school, you will also approach the SAT armed with examples from literature that may in turn suggest other examples from history or your personal experience. Two nights before the exam, I recommend that you read through your note cards on all the works that you've documented. Your approach to reviewing your documented readings should not be one of intense concentration. Rather, your approach should be one of relaxed confidence as you read through the cards because you've done the work and you would simply be refreshing your memory of what you've read. In summary, the more that you read and document those readings, the more examples will come to mind during the exam itself.

RECOMMENDED READING LIST

1. The Hero

The Iliad, Homer
The Odyssey, Homer
Metamorphoses, Ovid
The Aeneid, Virgil
Gilgamesh, (anon.)
Beowulf, (anon.)
Oedipus Rex, Sophocles

What it means to be a "hero" has evolved over time from the warrior with supernatural strength or the founder of a nation to a person of moral courage.

2. Conscience and Rights

A Man for All Seasons, Robert Bolt

After Being Convicted of Voting in the 1872 Presidential Election,
        Susan B. Anthony
The Life and Times of Frederick Douglass, Frederick Douglass
Letter from Birmingham Jail, Dr. Martin Luther King, Jr.
The Declaration of Independence, attributed to Thomas Jefferson
Resistance to Civil Government (Civil Disobedience)
        Thoreau
"Self-Reliance," Ralph Waldo Emerson
Adventures of Huckleberry Finn, Mark Twain
"For Passive Resisters," Mohandas Gandhi
Macbeth, William Shakespeare
"Shooting an Elephant," George Orwell

To Kill a Mockingbird, Harper Lee
The Things They Carried, Tim O'Brien

These select works treat the tension between an individual's conscience and the law or the expectations of others. Several also represent a "new kind of hero"—the hero of conscience.

3. Epiphanies

Emma, Jane Austen
Pride and Prejudice, Jane Austen
Dubliners, James Joyce (At a minimum, read "Araby" and "The Dead" in Joyce's collection of short stories.)

These three works are examples of characters' epiphanies—characters gaining unexpected insights into their flaws, faulty expectations, or moral blindness.

4. Effecting Change

David Copperfield, Charles Dickens
Narrative of the Life Of Frederick Douglass, an American Slave, Frederick Douglass
Uncle Tom's Cabin, or, Life Among the Lowly, Harriet Beecher Stowe.
The Jungle, Upton Sinclair
Silent Spring, Rachel Carson

These five works represent works in literature that offered social commentary or laid the groundwork for significant social change.

5. The American Dream

The Great Gatsby, F. Scott Fitzgerald
"Winter Dreams," F. Scott Fitzgerald
The Sun Also Rises, Ernest Hemingway
Death of a Salesman, Arthur Miller

6. Speeches

"Liberty or Death," Patrick Henry
"Gettysburg Address," Abraham Lincoln
"Inaugural Address," John Fitzgerald Kennedy
"Second Inaugural Address," Bill Clinton
"Funeral Oration," *Julius Caesar*, III.ii.79-113, William Shakespeare
"Treaty Oration," Chief Seattle

7. American Ethnic Writings

The Joy Luck Club, Amy Tan
Picture Bride, Yoshiko Uchida
Bury My Heart at Wounded Knee, Dee Brown
I Know Why the Caged Bird Sings, Maya Angelou
The Chosen, Chaim Potok
"No Name Woman," Maxine Hong Kingston
"The Way to Rainy Mountain," N. Scott Momaday
"The Myth of the Latin Woman: I Just Met a Girl Named Maria,"
        Judith Ortiz Cofer

8. Utopian/ Dystopian Literature

The Republic, Plato
Gulliver's Travels, (at a minimum, "Part IV: A Voyage to the
        Country of the Houyhnhnms"), Jonathan Swift
The History of Rasselas, Samuel Johnson
Animal Farm, George Orwell
1984, George Orwell
Fahrenheit 451, Ray Bradbury

9. American Southern Gothic

"A Rose for Emily," William Faulkner
"The Life You Save May Be Your Own," Flannery O'Connor
The Optimist's Daughter, Eudora Welty
The Heart is a Lonely Hunter, Carson McCullers

10. Miscellaneous

The Crucible, Henry Miller
The Scarlet Letter, Nathaniel Hawthorne
Tess of the D'Urbervilles, Thomas Hardy
My Antonia, Willa Cather
Lord of the Flies, William Golding
The Red Badge of Courage, Stephen Crane
Heart of Darkness, Joseph Conrad

APPENDIX A: SOME THOUGHTS ON STYLE

1. **Shorter is better.** If you're considering two ways to express a thought, choose the shorter version as long as the shorter version is *clear* (it says exactly what you want to say), *correct* (it has no grammatical errors), and *complete* (you communicate everything that you want to say about the topic). Now here's the same guideline in fewer words: five is better than fourteen.

2. **Prefer the dynamic to the static: prefer action verbs to linking verbs.** Action verbs are dynamic, even when the activity is mental, like thinking or deliberating. In contrast, linking verbs, which we went over in Lessons 1 and 11, are static; there's no movement or activity with them, not even intellectual movement. The verb "to be" is in reality an equal sign: "P.J. is the president of our student council." "P.J." equals or is the same as "our class president."Let's juxtapose (do I need to tell you what to do with that word?) two versions of a sentence—one with an action verb and one with a linking verb—and you can decide which version you would prefer to read or to write:

> A.   John is a man who provides for his family.
> B.   John provides for his family.

In Sentence A, the verb "is" is a linking verb, followed by a noun phrase, "a man," followed by the relative pronoun "who." There are more words in Sentence A than the writer needs to express a relatively simple idea. Sentence B, however, is much more to the point and more vigorous than Sentence A. Sentence B would be the preferred choice for a careful writer.

In a way, the choice between a static verb and an action verb is like deciding on a workout partner. If you wanted a workout partner who would motivate you to exercise, whom would you invite: the person who is always active or the couch potato? I think that you'd choose the active friend. Do the same with your verbs. [NOTE: This guideline doesn't mean that linking verbs have no place in effective writing. In fact, they are essential. We need linking verbs *am, are, is,* etc., to define terms, to inform others about the essential qualities of the people, places, or things that we're writing about. When I write, "My children are kind and generous," I am giving essential information about them, and I need the linking verb, in this case, "are," to make that statement. The same restriction applies to definitions, such as this one from the *New Oxford American Dictionary*: "rhetoric is the art of effective or persuasive speaking or writing, especially the use of figures of speech and other compositional techniques...." My point is that when **(but only when)** you have a *choice* between an action verb and a linking verb, prefer the action verb.]

3. **Prefer the active voice to the passive voice.** In *The Elements of Style*, Will Strunk says, "use the active voice," and gives several examples of his rule of composition. The example that I find especially useful is: "I shall always remember my first visit to Boston," which is much more "vigorous" than "my first visit to Boston will always be remembered by me." Authorities on style agree that sometimes a writer must use the passive voice, especially when the identity of the one who performed the action is unknown or unimportant. An example is, "Barriers had been placed along Constitution Avenue separating the spectators from the dignitaries who walked on the parade route." Do we really need to know the names or the titles of the people who placed the barriers? In this sentence, which uses the passive voice, the important point is not *who* placed the barriers on the parade route but *that barriers were there.* Here, in summary, is my guideline: when you have a legitimate choice between active and passive voice verbs, prefer the active voice to the passive. Your writing will be much more to the point and readable.

4. **Use a possessive before a gerund.** Even though it may sound a bit stiff and affected at times, correct grammar calls for the possessive case before a gerund. Remember that a gerund is a form of the verb that ends in "-ing" and acts like a noun, for example, "The audience at the talent show preferred my sister's singing to her guitar-playing." "Singing" and "guitar-playing" are

both gerunds behaving like nouns; in this case the gerunds are objects of the verb "preferred." In the example, I am following the rule: a possessive "my sister's" needs to precede "singing" and "guitar-playing." Note the correct idiom too: we say "preferred one thing *to* another thing," not "preferred one thing **over** another."]

5. **The rule for conjunctions.** When you want to join two independent clauses to form one sentence, you can do so with coordinating conjunctions (*for, and, nor, but, or, yet,* and *so*—the "good old" FANBOYS). In this option, you put a comma before one of the FANBOYS, and you have a correctly punctuated sentence, for example, "Henry Fielding was an attorney, but he still found time to write novels." Another way to join two independent clauses into one sentence is to use conjunctive adverbs. Here are some of the more common ones: *however, nevertheless, therefore, consequently,* and *moreover*. So we could also write: "Henry Fielding was a prolific novelist; however, he was still a practicing attorney."

Here are those examples for a closer comparison. (I'm using exaggerated spacing so that I can present the sentence's punctuation more clearly):

comma   *FANBOY*
↓   ↓
Henry Fielding was an attorney,   *but* he still found time to write novels.

semicolon   *conjunctive adverb*
↓   ↓
Henry Fielding was a prolific writer;   *however*   ,
he still practiced law.   ↑
                                            comma

6. It's acceptable, and at times preferred, to split initiatives. All too often, some of us English teachers will mount our hobbyhorses and wage a crusade against some offending word or phrase, leaving angry red comments in the margins of students' essays. The split infinitive rule is one such obsession. I'm sure that you've been told since elementary school not to split your infinitives. It is after all a "rule," isn't it? Well, let me share two things with you. First of all, some of the best authorities on style, grammar, and usage, don't consider this "rule" to be sacrosanct, a rule that's actually come down to us from 18th-century England.

At that time, when the scholars in England were compiling what they felt would be the definitive English grammar, they used Latin as their model. It's unlikely that anyone would have ever admitted it, but, for centuries, Latin had been considered superior to English. Latin was fixed and pristine. It had long been strictly a written language, so its rules were frozen in time. Additionally, while English was the common language, Latin had been the language of teachers, lawyers, churchmen, and members of the court. Being the language of the educated, Latin seemed to be a cut above English.

So when scholars forced the rules of Latin grammar upon the English language (what a bad decision that was) we inherited the ban against splitting infinitives. The grammarians' reasoning seemed unassailable at first glance, but it was flawed: an infinitive in Latin is one word, for example, *amare*, ("to love") or *videre* ("to see"), so it can't be split. Therefore, if you *can't split* an infinitive in Latin, you *may not split* one in English. Doesn't that reasoning seem a little feeble to you?

Authorities, with much higher credentials than many of us English teachers, however, have challenged that rule. The authorities say in effect that it's better not to split infinitives, but sometimes for sense or for the ease of constructing a sentence, a writer needs to split an infinitive. "The school had reason to believe from earlier hints that the alumnus, who had won the lottery, was going *to more than triple* his annual contributions to the university."[1] There doesn't seem to be any way around splitting the infinitive "to triple." Try placing the adverbial phrase, "more than," anywhere else in the sentence. Among the authorities who would offer some relief for the "split infinitive" rule are Bryan A. Gardner, author of the grammar-and-usage chapter of the *Chicago Manual of Style*, Will Strunk, whose guidelines many consider to be the gold standard for writing style, and Theodore M. Bernstein, former consulting editor of *The New York Times*. In *The Careful Writer*, Bernstein has the following to say about splitting infinitives, "there is nothing wrong with splitting an infinitive… except that eighteenth- and nineteenth-century grammarians… frowned on it. And most grammar teachers have been frowning ever since."

NOTE: There's one case in which it's much better NOT to split the infinitive. When you have an infinitive with a negative meaning, you should say or write, *"not to speak"* rather than "to not speak." It's preferred style and will satisfy all the split-infinitive hunters in classrooms and publishing houses, at least in this instance.

7. **Writing authorities assure us that we may end a clause with a preposition.** June Casagrande in *Grammar Snobs are Great Big Meanies: A Guide to Language for Fun and Spite* points out the absurdity of holding onto a rule that, if followed unfailingly, will lead to some rather silly sounding English, for instance, "pedantry up with which I will not put" attributed to Winston Churchill. To defy common sense and hold to this rule will satisfy some of us tightly-wound English teachers. On the other hand, authorities on style and grammar (look at the list of books that I recommend at the conclusion of *Relax I*) say it's perfectly acceptable to end a clause with a preposition. From my perspective, if ending a clause with a preposition is good enough for June Casagrande and other authorities, it ought to be good enough for you and me as well.

8. **Don't be overdressed.** Don't put on airs and be overly refined. (Think of the cheesy analogy in the text about wearing a suit to a

---

[1] Adapted from an example in Bernstein's *The Careful Writer*.

beach party. That's what the "between-you-and-I" error really is. Remember the "between-you-and-I" error and avoid it. The correct form of course is *between you and me* or *with James and me*.)

9. **Avoid piling up possessives.** You can avoid some awkward phrasing in your sentences by following this guideline. The following was part of a student's paper on Asia: "the Taliban's law's penalties." There's nothing wrong with the grammar, but two possessives with the same form—"'s"—are juxtaposed making the phrasing awkward. Try reading that excerpt aloud. It just doesn't sound very good. If we revise the wording just a bit, we can avoid piling up "'s" possessives. Possessives in English can take two different forms: an apostrophe with "s" or the prepositional phrase beginning with "of." We can take advantage of those options and produce a much smoother-sounding phrase: "the penalties of the Taliban's laws." Here's another example of awkward phrasing stemming from juxtaposing two "'s" possessives. "Shakespeare's family's financial difficulties prompted him to withdraw from the King's New School in Stratford." Revise that sentence to read, "the financial difficulties of Shakespeare's family prompted him to withdraw from the King's New School in Stratford." The revised sentence is much smoother.

10. **Write *"the reason that"* instead of "the reason why" or "the reason is because."** "The reason is because" and "the reason why" are redundant. The following sentence is the way to express the thought: "The reason that I must end this lesson is I am exhausted."

APPENDIX B: VOCABULARY

Did you look up these words from the text?

asinine	*defame*	*laudable*
ambiguity	*derision*	*ludicrous*
aspire	*egregious*	*mollify*
base	*ethos*	*profligate* [1]
bristle (verb)	*euphoric(ally)*	*sacrosanct*
circumvent	*fledgling*	*sporadic*
concession	*hobbyhorse*	*unassailable*
copious	*innate*	*unequivocally*
counterintuitive	*juxtapose*	*vilify*

A final word on vocabulary. Some of my students have made the mistake of trying to learn 20-30 vocabulary words a night! There's very little chance that anyone can sustain that pace or retain more than a fraction of the target words. Here's my suggestion: be realistic and COMMIT to learning five (5) vocabulary words daily. Look at the numbers: if you master five vocabulary words every day, you'll learn 35 words in a week and 140 words in a month. Following this approach and sticking to it, you will have added to your working vocabulary 700 words in five months.

Learning five vocabulary words every night is a manageable and realistic goal. That pace will allow you to retain vocabulary words in your short-term memory. With weekly review of your growing vocabulary, there's a much better chance that you'll retain more of the words in your long-term memory where they will be of lasting benefit to you. Remember that preparing for the SAT is a marathon, not a sprint. Pace yourself, and, as I said at the beginning, "relax." It's only five words. You'll do fine.

---

[1] "Profligate" appeared in an earlier version of *Relax.* It's a useful word. Look it up.

SAT RESOURCES I RECOMMEND

I deliberately avoided using the heading "Bibliography" for this section. When most readers see "Bibliography" at the top of a page, they don't give it a second thought and go back to reading the text without any feeling of guilt. Average readers don't pour over bibliographies anyway, nor do they track down some of the sources, and who would blame them? Bibliographies are necessary to ensure academic honesty for research and to give credit for information that we receive from others, but they don't always make for riveting reading. Throughout the text, I've cited my sources and given credit to the works that offer perfect examples for individual lessons or precise explanations of points of grammar and style. Now, I'd like to give you my comments on those books with just enough information to help you locate any book that appeals to you. By avoiding the term "Bibliography," I hope that you'll look at this list and consider some of these reference works that, as a writer and an editor, I have found not only very helpful but also highly enjoyable.

While there are a number of excellent SAT-preparation books for sale, I've included and commented on only the ones with which I have firsthand experience.

McGraw-Hill's *SAT: 6 Practice Tests, 2012 Edition*. This book is an excellent resource. It gives clear explanations of the various points of style and grammar that you will encounter on the SAT. The teaching points are reinforced with exercises. I especially liked the section on idioms. The only limitation for my money is that the book doesn't have more practice tests. (The McGraw-Hill SAT book is that good.)

College Board's The Official SAT Study Guide, Second Edition. In classical mythology, inquiring minds would consult an oracle to learn what the fates had dictated for the future, what dangers or good fortune lay ahead, whom and what to avoid or embrace, and what course of action to follow. The College Board's SAT-preparation book, with its ten practice tests, isn't exactly an oracle, but we should consider its practice tests as rock-solid indicators of the kinds of questions that will be on the exam. My students and I have used this book, and we've found it to be invaluable. The College Board, after all, is the sponsoring organization that oversees the development of the SATs each year. The book offers only a few points of instruction, and there are no explanations of the correct answers to the questions on the practice tests, but this book is essential because of the ten noteworthy practice tests.

Kaplan's *SAT 2010 Edition: Strategies, Practice, and Review*. This book offers excellent strategies on how to approach the questions and problems on the SAT's verbal and math sections. I like especially the book's suggestions for approaching the SAT essay. This book contains four practice tests with explanations of the answers; however, Kaplan also publishes *12 Practice Tests for the SAT: Maximum Practice for the SAT! 2012,* which offers more practice tests. By themselves or in combination, these books by Kaplan are worthwhile resources for your preparation work.

Bryan A. Garner's Modern American Usage, Third Edition, Oxford, is a gem. It's the final word on grammar and style. Check your semi-final drafts in high school and in college against this definitive work.

Barron's *SAT Critical Reading Workbook, 13th Edition; SAT Writing Workbook, 13th Edition;* and *SAT: Most Up-to-Date Review and Practice Tests Currently Available, 25th Edition.* I consider each one of these books a valuable resource. There are good explanations and exercises of the verbal problems to be expected on the SAT. My students and I have found these books to be very helpful.

Theodore M. Bernstein's *The Careful Writer: A Modern Guide to English Usage*, New York, Atheneum, 1986, is a terrific desk resource. His explanations of proper usage are authoritative, clear, and never stuffy. (He was, after all, an editor of the *New York Times* for years and a professor at Columbia University, so I for one listen to what he has to say very "carefully.") You're not going to read this book from cover to cover, but have it near your computer whenever you sit down to write an essay or a research paper. I like his sensible approach to and explanations of style and usage.

June Casagrande's *Grammar Snobs are Great Big Meanies: A Guide to Language for Fun and Spite*. This book is funny, readable, and sensible. It challenges some of the rigid and unnecessary rules that some of us tightly-wound English teachers have forced on our unwitting students for years. Like Bernstein's *The Careful Writer*, June Casagrande's *Grammar Snobs* is enjoyable to read and offers sensible dispensations for splitting infinitives and for ending clauses with prepositions when the prose actually would suffer from obeying the "rules."

Strunk and White's *The Elements of Style* is a book to own or to download on your computer. Will Strunk was E.B. White's English teacher when White was a freshman at Cornell University in the last century. Strunk gave his students a list of "rules" and guidelines that White compiled years later into *Elements*. This work is a classic and, in my view, is an easy-to-read reference for effective writing. Don't be surprised if you'll have to buy this book for your first-year English composition course. Even if you don't have to buy it, I would urge you to do so anyway and to put your copy of *Elements* within arm's reach whenever you start to write an essay or research paper. Also, I recommend that, every once in a while, you read, in one sitting, cover-to-cover, this easy-to-read book. (By the way, the book is much easier to read than that last sentence of mine.) Doing so and following its advice will help you improve your writing style. Anyway, what's 45 minutes out of 168 hours in your week or 45 minutes out of 672 hours in a month? Find the time to read it all the way through in one sitting. You won't regret it.

The St. Martin's Handbook, 5th Edition (Andrea A. Lunsford, principal author). This is a terrific reference book. It covers every conceivable grammatical error that you need to avoid. The explanations of the grammatical rules are clear with excellent examples. It also offers clear instruction on essay writing, effective style, and an explanation of how to conduct research and to document it properly in your academic papers. As with Bernstein's book and Strunk and White's classic, have the *St. Martin's Handbook* available when you sit down to write. I suggest finding a used copy to reduce the cost.

Virginia Tufte's *Artful Sentences: Syntax as Style*. Tufte's work is a delightful and wonderful compilation of more than a thousand well-crafted sentences from renowned authors of the twentieth and twenty-first centuries. The sentences can offer inspiration for both beginning and established authors. When we're looking to have "good sentences in our ears," this book is a great place to start. The book's introductory material also assures us that *Artful Sentences* is about models and successes—not "errors."

HUGE CAUTION FLAG

The SAT-preparation books that I've recommended are excellent; however, the term *caveat emptor* or "let the buyer beware" applies to SAT-preparation materials in general. Sometimes, publishers will offer the identical practice tests and material in subsequent editions of their SAT-preparation books. So, for instance, if you bought the 2013 version of a publisher's SAT-preparation book, make certain that the practice tests and exercises of any subsequent edition are in fact different from the one(s) you already have.

AFTERWORD

Well, we've come to the end. I have no doubt that you've worked carefully through the eighteen lessons on grammar and style and considered the guidance on SAT writing. Dedicated study (read *hard work*) produces knowledge, and knowledge fosters confidence. And with the confidence that you're gaining from *Relax I* and the follow-up work that I've recommended, you can approach the writing sections of the SAT poised and ready to do your best. And remember that your *honest* best (that is, when you've tried as hard as you can) is always good enough. You can do no better than your best.

So, relax. It's just SAT writing.

ABOUT THE AUTHOR

Dan Sullivan is an author and teacher who has worked for years helping students develop their writing skills and prepare for the SAT. His short stories have appeared in *World Wide Writers*, *New Millennium Writings*, and the annual short fiction anthologies of Scribes Valley Publishing.

Dan is a proud father and grandfather and lives in Southern Maryland with his wife Jamie.

www.ingramcontent.com/pod-product-compliance
Lightning Source LLC
LaVergne TN
LVHW051102080426
835508LV00019B/2028